THE DISCOURSE ON RIGHT VIEW

THE DISCOURSE ON RIGHT VIEW

The Sammādiṭṭhi Sutta
and its Commentary

Translated from the Pali by
Bhikkhu Ñāṇamoli

Edited and revised by
Bhikkhu Bodhi

BUDDHIST PUBLICATION SOCIETY
KANDY SRI LANKA

Published in 1991

Buddhist Publication Society
P.O. Box 61
54, Sangharaja Mawatha
Kandy, Sri Lanka

ISBN 955-24-0079-1

Typeset at the BPS
Text set in Garamond

Printed in Sri Lanka by
Karunaratne & Sons Ltd.
Colombo 10

THE WHEEL PUBLICATION NO. 377/379

Contents

Introduction 3

The Discourse on Right View 9

The Commentary to the Discourse on Right View 24

Notes 69

THE BUDDHA ON RIGHT VIEW

Bhikkhus, just as the dawn is the forerunner and first indication of the rising of the sun, so is right view the forerunner and first indication of wholesome states.

For one of right view, bhikkhus, right intention springs up. For one of right intention, right speech springs up. For one of right speech, right action springs up. For one of right action, right livelihood springs up. For one of right livelihood, right effort springs up. For one of right effort, right mindfulness springs up. For one of right mindfulness, right concentration springs up. For one of right concentration, right knowledge springs up. For one of right knowledge, right deliverance springs up.

Anguttara Nikāya 10:121

LIST OF ABBREVIATIONS

A.	Anguttara Nikāya
D.	Dīgha Nikāya
Dhp.	Dhammapada (by verse)
Dhs.	Dhammasangaṇī (by section)
M.	Majjhima Nikāya
S.	Saṁyutta Nikāya
Vibh.	Vibhanga

References to the Nikāyas cite the sutta number followed by the volume and page number of the Pali Text Society's roman script edition of the Pali text.

INTRODUCTION

The Sammādiṭṭhi Sutta, the Discourse on Right View, is the ninth sutta of the Majjhima Nikāya, the Collection of Middle Length Discourses. Its expositor is the Venerable Sāriputta Thera, the Buddha's chief disciple and the foremost of the Master's bhikkhu disciples in the exercise of the faculty of wisdom. The Buddha declared that next to himself, it was the Venerable Sāriputta who excelled in turning the incomparable Wheel of the Dhamma, in expounding in depth and in detail the Four Noble Truths realized with the attainment of enlightenment. In the Sammādiṭṭhi Sutta the great disciple bears ample testimony to the Buddha's words of praise, bequeathing upon us a discourse that has served as a primer of Buddhist doctrine for generations of monks in the monasteries of South and Southeast Asia.

As its title suggests, the subject of the Sammādiṭṭhi Sutta is right view. The analysis of right view undertaken in the sutta brings us to the very core of the Dhamma, since right view constitutes the correct understanding of the central teachings of the Buddha, the teachings which confer upon the Buddha's doctrine its own unique and distinctive stamp. Though the practice of right mindfulness has rightly been extolled as the crest jewel of the Buddha's teaching, it cannot be stressed strongly enough that the practice of mindfulness, or any other approach to meditation, only becomes an effective instrument of liberation to the extent that it is founded upon and guided by right view. Hence, to confirm the importance of right view, the Buddha places it at the very beginning of the Noble Eightfold Path. Elsewhere in the Suttas the Buddha calls right view the forerunner of the path (*pubbaṅgama*), which gives direction and efficacy to the other seven path factors.

Right view, as explained in the commentary to the Sammādiṭṭhi Sutta, has a variety of aspects, but it might best be considered as twofold: *conceptual right view*, which is the intellectual grasp of the principles enunciated in the Buddha's teaching, and *experiential right view*, which is the wisdom that arises by direct penetration of the teaching. Conceptual right view, also called the right view in conformity with the truths (*saccānulomika-sammādiṭṭhi*), is a correct conceptual understanding of the Dhamma arrived at by study of the Buddha's teachings and deep examination of their meaning. Such understanding, though conceptual rather than experiential, is not dry and sterile. When rooted in faith in the Triple Gem and driven by a keen aspiration to realize the truth embedded in the formulated principles of the Dhamma, it serves as a critical phase in the development of wisdom (*paññā*), for it provides the germ out of which experiential right view gradually evolves.

Experiential right view is the penetration of the truth of the teaching in one's own immediate experience. Thus it is also called right view that penetrates the truths (*saccapaṭivedha-sammādiṭṭhi*). This type of right view is aroused by the practice of insight meditation guided by a correct conceptual understanding of the Dhamma. To arrive at direct penetration, one must begin with a correct conceptual grasp of the teaching and transform that grasp from intellectual comprehension to direct perception by cultivating the threefold training in morality, concentration and wisdom. If conceptual right view can be compared to a hand, a hand that grasps the truth by way of concepts, then experiential right view can be compared to an eye—the eye of wisdom that sees directly into the true nature of existence ordinarily hidden from us by our greed, aversion and delusion.

The Discourse on Right View is intended to elucidate the

principles that are to be comprehended by conceptual right view and penetrated by experiential right view. The Venerable Sāriputta expounds these principles under sixteen headings: the wholesome and the unwholesome, the four nutriments of life, the Four Noble Truths, the twelve factors of dependent arising, and the taints as the condition for ignorance. It will be noted that from the second section to the end of the sutta, all the expositions are framed in accordance with the same structure, which reveals the principle of conditionality as the scaffolding for the entire teaching. Each phenomenon to be comprehended by right view is expounded in terms of its individual nature, its arising, its cessation, and the way leading to its cessation. The grasp of this principle thus makes it clear that any entity taken for examination is not an isolated occurrence with its being locked up in itself, but part of a web of conditionally arisen processes that can be terminated by understanding and eliminating the cause that gives it being.

The right view arrived at by penetrating any of the sixteen subjects expounded in the sutta is discussed in terms of two aspects, both aspects of supramundane penetration. The first is the initial penetration of the supramundane path that transforms a person from a worldling (*puthujjana*) into a stream-enterer (*sotāpanna*), a noble disciple who has entered irreversibly upon the stream to liberation. This aspect of right view is indicated by the words that open each section, "(one) who has perfect confidence in the Dhamma and has arrived at this true Dhamma." These qualities are attributes only of the stream-enterer and those of higher attainment along the path. The description thus applies to the trainee (*sekha*), the disciple who has entered the path but has not yet reached its end. The words signify right view as a transformative vision which has revealed the ultimate truths underlying our existence, but which must still be developed further to complete the full transformation it is capable of effecting.

The second aspect of supramundane right view is indicated by the closing words of each section, from "he entirely abandons the underlying tendency to lust" to "he here and now makes an end of suffering." This description is fully applicable only to the Arahant, the liberated one, and thus indicates that the right view conceptually grasped by the wise worldling, and transformed into direct perception with the attainment of stream-entry, reaches its consummation with the arrival at the teaching's final goal, the attainment of complete emancipation from suffering.

* * *

The translation of the Sammādiṭṭhi Sutta and its commentary presented here has been adapted from manuscripts left behind by Bhikkhu Ñāṇamoli. The translation of the sutta has been adapted from Ven. Ñāṇamoli's complete translation of the Majjhima Nikāya. The version used has been taken from the edition of the complete Majjhima Nikāya translation that I prepared for publication by Wisdom Publications in the United States. This version, tentatively scheduled for release in late 1992, employs extensive substitution of Ven. Ñāṇamoli's own technical terminology with my own preferred renderings of Pali doctrinal terms.

The commentary to the Sammādiṭṭhi Sutta is from the *Papañcasūdanī*, Ācariya Buddhaghosa's complete commentary (*aṭṭhakathā*) to the Majjhima Nikāya. The translation of the commentary has also been adapted from a rendering by Ven. Ñāṇamoli, contained in a notebook of his that was discovered only a few years ago at Island Hermitage. The terminology used in the notebook version suggests that it was one of Ven. Ñāṇamoli's earliest attempts at translation from the Pali; it certainly preceded his translation of the *Visuddhimagga*, *The Path of Purification*, first completed at the end of 1953. In adapting the translation, I have naturally replaced the technical terminology used in the notebook version with that used in the sutta. In places I also decided to translate directly from the Pali text rather than adhere to Ven. Ñāṇamoli's rendering, which sometimes tended to be literal to the point of awkwardness. A few passages from the commentary that are concerned solely with linguistic clarification have been omitted from the translation.

Passages in the commentarial section enclosed in square brackets are taken from the subcommentary to the Sammādiṭṭhi Sutta, by Ācariya Dhammapāla. Passages in parenthesis are additions either by Ven. Ñāṇamoli or by myself. The paragraph numbering of the commentarial section follows that of the sutta. The phrases of the sutta that are selected for comment have been set in boldface. The backnotes are entirely my own.

BHIKKHU BODHI

PART ONE
THE DISCOURSE ON RIGHT VIEW
(*Sammādiṭṭhi Sutta*)

1. Thus have I heard. On one occasion the Blessed One was living at Sāvatthī in Jeta's Grove, Anāthapiṇḍika's Park. There the Venerable Sāriputta addressed the bhikkhus thus: "Friends, bhikkhus."—"Friend," they replied. The Venerable Sāriputta said this:

2. "'One of right view, one of right view' is said, friends. In what way is a noble disciple one of right view, whose view is straight, who has perfect confidence in the Dhamma, and has arrived at this true Dhamma?"

"Indeed, friend, we would come from far away to learn from the Venerable Sāriputta the meaning of this statement. It would be good if the Venerable Sāriputta would explain the meaning of this statement. Having heard it from him, the bhikkhus will remember it."

"Then, friends, listen and attend closely to what I shall say."

"Yes, friend," the bhikkhus replied. The Venerable Sāriputta said this:

The Wholesome and the Unwholesome

3. "When, friends, a noble disciple understands the unwholesome, the root of the unwholesome, the wholesome, and the root of the wholesome, in that way he is one of right view, whose view is straight, who has perfect confidence in the Dhamma, and has arrived at this true Dhamma.

4. "And what, friends, is the unwholesome, what is the root of

the unwholesome, what is the wholesome, what is the root of the wholesome? Killing living beings is unwholesome; taking what is not given is unwholesome; misconduct in sensual pleasures is unwholesome; false speech is unwholesome; malicious speech is unwholesome; harsh speech is unwholesome; gossip is unwholesome; covetousness is unwholesome; ill will is unwholesome; wrong view is unwholesome. This is called the unwholesome.

5. "And what is the root of the unwholesome? Greed is a root of the unwholesome; hate is a root of the unwholesome; delusion is a root of the unwholesome. This is called the root of the unwholesome.

6. "And what is the wholesome? Abstention from killing living beings is wholesome; abstention from taking what is not given is wholesome; abstention from misconduct in sensual pleasures is wholesome; abstention from false speech is wholesome; abstention from malicious speech is wholesome; abstention from harsh speech is wholesome; abstention from gossip is wholesome; non-covetousness is wholesome; non-ill will is wholesome; right view is wholesome. This is called the wholesome.

7. "And what is the root of the wholesome? Non-greed is a root of the wholesome; non-hate is a root of the wholesome; non-delusion is a root of the wholesome. This is called the root of the wholesome.

8. "When a noble disciple has thus understood the unwholesome, the root of the unwholesome, the wholesome, and the root of the wholesome, he entirely abandons the underlying tendency to lust, he abolishes the underlying tendency to aversion, he extirpates the underlying tendency to the view and conceit 'I am,' and by abandoning ignorance and arousing true knowledge he here and now makes an end of suffering. In that way too a noble disciple is one of right view, whose view is straight, who has perfect confidence in the Dhamma and has arrived at this true Dhamma."

Nutriment

9. Saying, "Good, friend," the bhikkhus delighted and rejoiced in the Venerable Sāriputta's words. Then they asked him a further question: "But, friend, might there be another way in which a noble disciple is one of right view ... and has arrived at this true Dhamma?"—"There might be, friends.

10. "When, friends, a noble disciple understands nutriment, the origin of nutriment, the cessation of nutriment, and the way leading to the cessation of nutriment, in that way he is one of right view ... and has arrived at this true Dhamma.

11. "And what is nutriment, what is the origin of nutriment, what is the cessation of nutriment, what is the way leading to the cessation of nutriment? There are these four kinds of nutriment for the maintenance of beings that already have come to be and for the support of those seeking a new existence. What four? They are physical food as nutriment, gross or subtle; contact as the second; mental volition as the third; and consciousness as the fourth. With the arising of craving there is the arising of nutriment. With the cessation of craving there is the cessation of nutriment. The way leading to the cessation of nutriment is just this Noble Eightfold Path; that is, right view, right intention, right speech, right action, right livelihood, right effort, right mindfulness and right concentration.

12. "When a noble disciple has thus understood nutriment, the origin of nutriment, the cessation of nutriment, and the way leading to the cessation of nutriment, he entirely abandons the underlying tendency to greed, he abolishes the underlying tendency to aversion, he extirpates the underlying tendency to the view and conceit 'I am,' and by abandoning ignorance and arousing true knowledge he here and now makes an end of suffering. In that way too a noble disciple is one of right view, whose view is straight, who has perfect confidence in the Dhamma and has arrived at this true Dhamma."

The Four Noble Truths

13. Saying, "Good, friend," the bhikkhus delighted and rejoiced in the Venerable Sāriputta's words. Then they asked him a further question: "But, friend, might there be another way in which a noble disciple is one of right view … and has arrived at this true Dhamma?"—"There might be, friends.

14. "When, friends, a noble disciple understands suffering, the origin of suffering, the cessation of suffering, and the way leading to the cessation of suffering, in that way he is one of right view … and has arrived at this true Dhamma.

15. "And what is suffering, what is the origin of suffering, what is the cessation of suffering, what is the way leading to the cessation of suffering? Birth is suffering; ageing is suffering; sickness is suffering; death is suffering; sorrow, lamentation, pain, grief and despair are suffering; not to obtain what one wants is suffering; in short, the five aggregates affected by clinging are suffering. This is called suffering.

16. "And what is the origin of suffering? It is craving, which brings renewal of being, is accompanied by delight and lust, and delights in this and that; that is, craving for sensual pleasures, craving for being and craving for non-being. This is called the origin of suffering.

17. "And what is the cessation of suffering? It is the remainderless fading away and ceasing, the giving up, relinquishing, letting go and rejecting of that same craving. This is called the cessation of suffering.

18. "And what is the way leading to the cessation of suffering? It is just this Noble Eightfold Path; that is, right view … right concentration. This is called the way leading to the cessation of suffering.

19. "When a noble disciple has thus understood suffering, the origin of suffering, the cessation of suffering, and the way leading to the cessation of suffering … he here and now makes

an end of suffering. In that way too a noble disciple is one of right view ... and has arrived at this true Dhamma."

Ageing and Death

20. Saying, "Good, friend," the bhikkhus delighted and rejoiced in the Venerable Sāriputta's words. Then they asked him a further question: "But, friend, might there be another way in which a noble disciple is one of right view ... and has arrived at this true Dhamma?"—"There might be, friends.

21. "When, friends, a noble disciple understands ageing and death, the origin of ageing and death, the cessation of ageing and death, and the way leading to the cessation of ageing and death, in that way he is one of right view ... and has arrived at this true Dhamma.

22. "And what is ageing and death, what is the origin of ageing and death, what is the cessation of ageing and death, what is the way leading to the cessation of ageing and death? The ageing of beings in the various orders of beings, their old age, brokenness of teeth, greyness of hair, wrinkling of skin, decline of life, weakness of faculties—this is called ageing. The passing of beings out of the various orders of beings, their passing away, dissolution, disappearance, dying, completion of time, dissolution of the aggregates, laying down of the body—this is called death. So this ageing and this death are what is called ageing and death. With the arising of birth there is the arising of ageing and death. With the cessation of birth there is the cessation of ageing and death. The way leading to the cessation of ageing and death is just this Noble Eightfold Path; that is, right view ... right concentration.

23. "When a noble disciple has thus understood ageing and death, the origin of ageing and death, the cessation of ageing and death, and the way leading to the cessation of ageing and death ... he here and now makes an end of suffering. In that

way too a noble disciple is one of right view ... and has arrived at this true Dhamma."

Birth

24. Saying, "Good, friend," the bhikkhus delighted and rejoiced in the Venerable Sāriputta's words. Then they asked him a further question: "But, friend, might there be another way in which a noble disciple is one of right view ... and has arrived at this true Dhamma?"—"There might be, friends.

25. "When, friends, a noble disciple understands birth, the origin of birth, the cessation of birth, and the way leading to the cessation of birth, in that way he is one of right view ... and has arrived at this true Dhamma.

26. "And what is birth, what is the origin of birth, what is the cessation of birth, what is the way leading to the cessation of birth? The birth of beings into the various orders of beings, their coming to birth, precipitation (in a womb), generation, manifestation of the aggregates, obtaining the bases for contact—this is called birth. With the arising of being there is the arising of birth. With the cessation of being there is the cessation of birth. The way leading to the cessation of birth is just this Noble Eightfold Path; that is, right view ... right concentration.

27. "When a noble disciple has thus understood birth, the origin of birth, the cessation of birth, and the way leading to the cessation of birth ... he here and now makes an end of suffering. In that way too a noble disciple is one of right view ... and has arrived at this true Dhamma."

Being

28. Saying, "Good, friend," the bhikkhus delighted and rejoiced in the Venerable Sāriputta's words. Then they asked him a further question: "But, friend, might there be another way in

which a noble disciple is one of right view ... and has arrived at this true Dhamma?"— "There might be, friends.

29. "When, friends, a noble disciple understands being, the origin of being, the cessation of being, and the way leading to the cessation of being, in that way he is one of right view ... and has arrived at this true Dhamma.

30. "And what is being, what is the origin of being, what is the cessation of being, what is the way leading to the cessation of being? There are these three kinds of being: sense-sphere being, fine-material being and immaterial being. With the arising of clinging there is the arising of being. With the cessation of clinging there is the cessation of being. The way leading to the cessation of being is just this Noble Eightfold Path; that is, right view ... right concentration.

31. "When a noble disciple has thus understood being, the origin of being, the cessation of being, and the way leading to the cessation of being ... he here and now makes an end of suffering. In that way too a noble disciple is one of right view ... and has arrived at this true Dhamma."

Clinging

32. Saying, "Good, friend," the bhikkhus delighted and rejoiced in the Venerable Sāriputta's words. Then they asked him a further question: "But, friend, might there be another way in which a noble disciple is one of right view ... and has arrived at this true Dhamma?"—"There might be, friends.

33. "When, friends, a noble disciple understands clinging, the origin of clinging, the cessation of clinging, and the way leading to the cessation of clinging, in that way he is one of right view ... and has arrived at this true Dhamma.

34. "And what is clinging, what is the origin of clinging, what is the cessation of clinging, what is the way leading to the cessation of clinging? There are these four kinds of clinging:

clinging to sensual pleasures, clinging to views, clinging to rituals and observances, and clinging to a doctrine of self. With the arising of craving there is the arising of clinging. With the cessation of craving there is the cessation of clinging. The way leading to the cessation of clinging is just this Noble Eightfold Path; that is, right view ... right concentration.

35. "When a noble disciple has thus understood clinging, the origin of clinging, the cessation of clinging, and the way leading to the cessation of clinging ... he here and now makes an end of suffering. In that way too a noble disciple is one of right view ... and has arrived at this true Dhamma."

Craving

36. Saying, "Good, friend," the bhikkhus delighted and rejoiced in the Venerable Sāriputta's words. Then they asked him a further question: "But, friend, might there be another way in which a noble disciple is one of right view ... and has arrived at this true Dhamma?"—"There might be, friends.

37. "When, friends, a noble disciple understands craving, the origin of craving, the cessation of craving, and the way leading to the cessation of craving, in that way he is one of right view ... and has arrived at this true Dhamma.

38. "And what is craving, what is the origin of craving, what is the cessation of craving, what is the way leading to the cessation of craving? There are these six classes of craving: craving for forms, craving for sounds, craving for odours, craving for flavours, craving for tangibles, craving for mind-objects. With the arising of feeling there is the arising of craving. With the cessation of feeling there is the cessation of craving. The way leading to the cessation of craving is just this Noble Eightfold Path; that is, right view ... right concentration.

39. "When a noble disciple has thus understood craving, the origin of craving, the cessation of craving, and the way leading

to the cessation of craving ... he here and now makes an end of suffering. In that way too a noble disciple is one of right view ... and has arrived at this true Dhamma."

Feeling

40. Saying, "Good, friend," the bhikkhus delighted and rejoiced in the Venerable Sāriputta's words. Then they asked him a further question: "But, friend, might there be another way in which a noble disciple is one of right view ... and has arrived at this true Dhamma?"—"There might be, friends.

41. "When, friends, a noble disciple understands feeling, the origin of feeling, the cessation of feeling, and the way leading to the cessation of feeling, in that way he is one of right view ... and has arrived at this true Dhamma.

42. "And what is feeling, what is the origin of feeling, what is the cessation of feeling, what is the way leading to the cessation of feeling? There are these six classes of feeling: feeling born of eye-contact, feeling born of ear-contact, feeling born of nose-contact, feeling born of tongue-contact, feeling born of body-contact, feeling born of mind-contact. With the arising of contact there is the arising of feeling. With the cessation of contact there is the cessation of feeling. The way leading to the cessation of feeling is just this Noble Eightfold Path; that is, right view ... right concentration.

43. "When a noble disciple has thus understood feeling, the origin of feeling, the cessation of feeling, and the way leading to the cessation of feeling ... he here and now makes an end of suffering. In that way too a noble disciple is one of right view ... and has arrived at this true Dhamma."

Contact

44. Saying, "Good, friend," the bhikkhus delighted and rejoiced in the Venerable Sāriputta's words. Then they asked him

a further question: "But, friend, might there be another way in which a noble disciple is one of right view ... and has arrived at this true Dhamma?"—"There might be, friends.

45. "When, friends, a noble disciple understands contact, the origin of contact, the cessation of contact, and the way leading to the cessation of contact, in that way he is one of right view ... and has arrived at this true Dhamma.

46. "And what is contact, what is the origin of contact, what is the cessation of contact, what is the way leading to the cessation of contact? There are these six classes of contact: eye-contact, ear-contact, nose-contact, tongue-contact, body-contact, mind-contact. With the arising of the sixfold base there is the arising of contact. With the cessation of the sixfold base there is the cessation of contact. The way leading to the cessation of contact is just this Noble Eightfold Path; that is, right view ... right concentration.

47. "When a noble disciple has thus understood contact, the origin of contact, the cessation of contact, and the way leading to the cessation of contact ... he here and now makes an end of suffering. In that way too a noble disciple is one of right view ... and has arrived at this true Dhamma."

The Sixfold Base

48. Saying, "Good, friend," the bhikkhus delighted and rejoiced in the Venerable Sāriputta's words. Then they asked him a further question: "But, friend, might there be another way in which a noble disciple is one of right view ... and has arrived at this true Dhamma?"—"There might be, friends.

49. "When, friends, a noble disciple understands the sixfold base, the origin of the sixfold base, the cessation of the sixfold base, and the way leading to the cessation of the sixfold base, he is one of right view ... and has arrived at this true Dhamma.

50. "And what is the sixfold base, what is the origin of the

sixfold base, what is the cessation of the sixfold base, what is the way leading to the cessation of the sixfold base? There are these six bases: the eye-base, the ear-base, the nose-base, the tongue-base, the body-base, the mind-base. With the arising of mentality-materiality there is the arising of the sixfold base. With the cessation of mentality-materiality there is the cessation of the sixfold base. The way leading to the cessation of the sixfold base is just this Noble Eightfold Path; that is, right view ... right concentration.

51. "When a noble disciple has thus understood the sixfold base, the origin of the sixfold base, the cessation of the sixfold base, and the way leading to the cessation of the sixfold base ... he here and now makes an end of suffering. In that way too a noble disciple is one of right view ... and has arrived at this true Dhamma."

Mentality-Materiality

52. Saying, "Good, friend," the bhikkhus delighted and rejoiced in the Venerable Sāriputta's words. Then they asked him a further question: "But, friend, might there be another way in which a noble disciple is one of right view ... and has arrived at this true Dhamma?"—"There might be, friends.

53. "When, friends, a noble disciple understands mentality-materiality, the origin of mentality-materiality, the cessation of mentality-materiality, and the way leading to the cessation of mentality-materiality, in that way he is one of right view ... and has arrived at this true Dhamma.

54. "And what is mentality-materiality, what is the origin of mentality-materiality, what is the cessation of mentality-materiality, what is the way leading to the cessation of mentality-materiality? Feeling, perception, volition, contact and attention—these are called mentality. The four great elements and the material form derived from the four great elements—these

are called materiality. So this mentality and this materiality are what is called mentality-materiality. With the arising of consciousness there is the arising of mentality-materiality. With the cessation of consciousness there is the cessation of mentality-materiality. The way leading to the cessation of mentality-materiality is just this Noble Eightfold Path; that is, right view ... right concentration.

55. "When a noble disciple has thus understood mentality-materiality, the origin of mentality-materiality, the cessation of mentality-materiality, and the way leading to the cessation of mentality-materiality ... he here and now makes an end of suffering. In that way too a noble disciple is one of right view ... and has arrived at this true Dhamma."

Consciousness

56. Saying, "Good, friend," the bhikkhus delighted and rejoiced in the Venerable Sāriputta's words. Then they asked him a further question: "But, friend, might there be another way in which a noble disciple is one of right view ... and has arrived at this true Dhamma?"—"There might be, friends.

57. "When, friends, a noble disciple understands consciousness, the origin of consciousness, the cessation of consciousness, and the way leading to the cessation of consciousness, in that way he is one of right view ... and has arrived at this true Dhamma.

58. "And what is consciousness, what is the origin of consciousness, what is the cessation of consciousness, what is the way leading to the cessation of consciousness? There are these six classes of consciousness: eye-consciousness, ear-consciousness, nose-consciousness, tongue-consciousness, body-consciousness, mind-consciousness. With the arising of formations there is the arising of consciousness. With the cessation of formations there is the cessation of consciousness. The way leading to the cessa-

tion of consciousness is just this Noble Eightfold Path; that is, right view ... right concentration.

59. "When a noble disciple has thus understood consciousness, the origin of consciousness, the cessation of consciousness, and the way leading to the cessation of consciousness ... he here and now makes an end of suffering. In that way too a noble disciple is one of right view ... and has arrived at this true Dhamma."

Formations

60. Saying, "Good friend," the bhikkhus delighted and rejoiced in the Venerable Sāriputta's words. Then they asked him a further question: "But, friend, might there be another way in which a noble disciple is one of right view ... and has arrived at this true Dhamma?"—"There might be, friends.

61. "When, friends, a noble disciple understands formations, the origin of formations, the cessation of formations, and the way leading to the cessation of formations, in that way he is one of right view ... and has arrived at this true Dhamma.

62. "And what are formations, what is the origin of formations, what is the cessation of formations, what is the way leading to the cessation of formations? There are these three kinds of formations: the bodily formation, the verbal formation, the mental formation. With the arising of ignorance there is the arising of formations. With the cessation of ignorance there is the cessation of formations. The way leading to the cessation of formations is just this Noble Eightfold Path; that is, right view ... right concentration.

63. "When a noble disciple has thus understood formations, the origin of formations, the cessation of formations, and the way leading to the cessation of formations ... he here and now makes an end of suffering. In that way too a noble disciple is one of right view ... and has arrived at this true Dhamma."

Ignorance

64. Saying, "Good friend," the bhikkhus delighted and rejoiced in the Venerable Sāriputta's words. Then they asked him a further question: "But, friend, might there be another way in which a noble disciple is one of right view ... and has arrived at this true Dhamma?"—"There might be, friends.

65. "When, friends, a noble disciple understands ignorance, the origin of ignorance, the cessation of ignorance, and the way leading to the cessation of ignorance, in that way he is one of right view ... and has arrived at this true Dhamma.

66. "And what is ignorance, what is the origin of ignorance, what is the cessation of ignorance, what is the way leading to the cessation of ignorance? Not knowing about suffering, not knowing about the origin of suffering, not knowing about the cessation of suffering, not knowing about the way leading to the cessation of suffering—this is called ignorance. With the arising of the taints there is the arising of ignorance. With the cessation of the taints there is the cessation of ignorance. The way leading to the cessation of ignorance is just this Noble Eightfold Path; that is, right view ... right concentration.

67. "When a noble disciple has thus understood ignorance, the origin of ignorance, the cessation of ignorance, and the way leading to the cessation of ignorance ... he here and now makes an end of suffering. In that way too a noble disciple is one of right view ... and has arrived at this true Dhamma."

Taints

68. Saying, "Good, friend," the bhikkhus delighted and rejoiced in the Venerable Sāriputta's words. Then they asked him a further question: "But, friend, might there be another way in which a noble disciple is one of right view, whose view is straight, who has perfect confidence in the Dhamma and has arrived at this true Dhamma?"— "There might be, friends.

69. "When, friends, a noble disciple understands the taints, the origin of the taints, the cessation of the taints, and the way leading to the cessation of the taints, in that way he is one of right view, whose view is straight, who has perfect confidence in the Dhamma and has arrived at this true Dhamma.

70. "And what are the taints, what is the origin of the taints, what is the cessation of the taints, what is the way leading to the cessation of the taints? There are three taints: the taint of sensual desire, the taint of being and the taint of ignorance. With the arising of ignorance there is the arising of the taints. With the cessation of ignorance there is the cessation of the taints. The way leading to the cessation of the taints is just this Noble Eightfold Path; that is, right view, right intention, right speech, right action, right livelihood, right effort, right mindfulness and right concentration.

71. "When a noble disciple has thus understood the taints, the origin of the taints, the cessation of the taints, and the way leading to the cessation of the taints, he entirely abandons the underlying tendency to lust, he abolishes the underlying tendency to aversion, he extirpates the underlying tendency to the view and conceit 'I am,' and by abandoning ignorance and arousing true knowledge he here and now makes an end of suffering. In that way too a noble disciple is one of right view, whose view is straight, who has perfect confidence in the Dhamma and has arrived at this true Dhamma."

That is what the Venerable Sāriputta said. The bhikkhus were satisfied and delighted in the Venerable Sāriputta's words.

PART TWO

THE COMMENTARY TO THE DISCOURSE ON RIGHT VIEW

1. **Thus have I heard:** the Sammādiṭṭhi Sutta.

2. Herein, all such questions spoken by the Elder as " 'One of right view, one of right view' is said, friends. In what way is a noble disciple one of right view ...?" or "And what, friends, is the unwholesome ...?"—these are questions showing a desire to expound. Herein, since those who know, those who do not know, those outside the Dispensation, those within it, those who speak by hearsay, etc., and those who speak by personal knowledge, say "one of right view," therefore, taking it as an expression (common) to the many, he touched upon it twice, saying **"One of right view, one of right view" is said, friends** (*sammādiṭṭhi sammādiṭṭhī ti āvuso vuccati*). The intention here is this: "Others say 'one of right view,' and still others say 'one of right view.' Since that is said, in what way, friends, is a noble disciple one of right view in respect of meaning and characteristic?" Herein, **one of right view** is one possessing a lucid and praiseworthy view (*sobhanāya pasatthāya ca diṭṭhiyā samannāgato*). But when this word "right view" is used to signify a state (rather than a person endowed with that state), it then means a lucid and praiseworthy view.[1]

This right view is twofold: **mundane** (*lokiya*) and **supramundane** (*lokuttara*). Herein, the knowledge of kamma as one's own and knowledge which is in conformity with the (Four Noble) Truths are **mundane right view**; or, in brief, (mundane right view is) all understanding that is accompanied by the taints.[2] Understanding connected with the noble paths and fruits is **supramundane right view.**[3] The person possessing right view is of three kinds: the worldling (*puthujjana*), the disciple in higher training (*sekha*), and the one beyond training (*asekha*). Herein, the worldling is of two kinds: one outside the Dispensation and one within the Dispensation. Herein, one outside the Dispensation who believes in kamma is one of right view on account of the view of kamma as one's own, but not on account of that which is in conformity with the truths, because he holds to the view of self. One within the Dispensation is of right view on account of both. The disciple in higher training is one of right view on account of fixed right view,[4] the one beyond training on account of (the right view) that is beyond training.[5]

But here "one of right view" is intended as one possessing supramundane wholesome right view, which is fixed in destiny and emancipating. Hence he said: **whose view is straight, who has perfect confidence in the Dhamma, and has arrived at this true Dhamma** (*ujugatā'ssa diṭṭhi dhamme aveccappasādena samannāgato āgato imaṁ saddhammaṁ*). Because of its going straight without deviating to either extreme, or because of its going straight by removing all crookedness such as bodily crookedness, etc., supramundane right view is "straight." One possessing that view also possesses perfect confidence, unshakable confidence, in the ninefold supramundane Dhamma.[6] And by becoming disentangled from all the thickets of (wrong) views, by abandoning all the defilements, by departing from the round of rebirths, by bringing the practice to its consummation, he is said to have come by the noble path to this "true Dhamma" proclaimed by the Enlightened One, that is, Nibbāna, the plunge into the Deathless.

The Wholesome and the Unwholesome

3. **Understands the unwholesome** (*akusalañ ca pajānāti*): he understands the unwholesome called the ten courses of unwholesome kamma (action), penetrating this by way of function with the understanding that has Nibbāna as its object as "This is suffering." **(Understands) the root of the unwholesome** (*akusalamūlañ ca pajānāti*): And he understands the unwholesome root which has become the root condition of that (unwholesome), penetrating this, in the same way, as "This is the origin of suffering." The same method applies here also in regard to "the wholesome" and "the root of the wholesome." And, as it is here, so in all the following sections, the understanding of the subject should be understood by way of function.

In that way (*ettāvatā pi*): by this much; by this understanding of the unwholesome, etc. **He is one of right view** (*sammādiṭṭhi hoti*): he possesses supramundane right view of the kind aforesaid. **Whose view is straight ... and has arrived at this true Dhamma:** At this point the summary version of the teaching has been expounded. And this (part of) the teaching itself was brief; but for those bhikkhus it should be understood that the penetration (of the meaning) through right attention occurred in detail.

But in the second section (§4) it should be understood that the teaching too, as well as the penetration through attention, is stated in detail.

Herein, the bhikkhus [at the council at the Great Monastery held to rehearse the Pitakas] said: "In the brief exposition the two lower paths are discussed, in the detailed exposition the two higher paths," taking into account the passage at the end of the sections setting forth the detailed exposition that begins "he entirely abandons the underlying tendency to lust." But the Elder (presiding over the council) said: "In the brief exposition the four paths are expounded as a group, and also in the detailed exposition."[7]

This query into the brief and detailed expositions which has been cleared up here should be understood in all the following sections in the way stated here. From here on we shall only comment on terms that are new or obscure.

The Unwholesome Courses of Action

4. Herein, firstly, in the detailed exposition of the first section: as regards the passage beginning **killing living beings is unwholesome** (*pāṇātipāto kho āvuso akusalaṁ*), "unwholesome" should be understood by way of the occurrence of unwholesomeness, or as what is opposed to the wholesome, which is to be dealt with below (§6). As to characteristic, it is blameworthy and has painful result, or it is defiled. This, in the first place, is the comment upon the general terms here.

But as regards the particular terms, the phrase **killing living beings** means the slaughter of a living being, the destruction of a living being. And here **a living being** (*pāṇa*) is, according to ordinary usage, a being (*satta*); in the ultimate sense it is the life faculty. "Killing living beings" is the volition to kill on the part of one who is aware, in respect of a living being, that it is a living being, and which (volition), manifesting itself through one or the other of the doors of body and speech, initiates activity resulting in the cutting off of the life faculty.

In relation to beings such as animals, etc., which lack moral qualities (*guṇa*), it is less blameworthy in respect of small living beings and more blameworthy in respect of beings with large bodies. Why? Because of the magnitude of the effort involved. And when the effort involved is equal, because of the magnitude of the object (the being killed). In relation to beings such as humans, etc., who possess moral qualities, it is less blameworthy in respect of beings with few good qualities and more blameworthy in respect of beings with great qualities. When the size of the body and moral qualities are equal, however, it is less blameworthy when the defilements and activity are mild, and more blameworthy when they are strong: so it should be understood.

There are five constituents for this (act of killing a living being): a living being, awareness that it is a living being, the mind to kill, activity, and the death (of the being) thereby.

There are six means: one's own person, command, a missile, a fixed contrivance, a magical spell, supernormal power.

To explore this matter in detail, however, would involve too much diffuseness. Therefore we shall not explore it in detail, or any other subject similar in kind. Those who wish to go into the matter may do so by looking it up in the *Samantapāsādikā*, the Vinaya Commentary.[8]

Taking what is not given (*adinnādāna*): the carrying off of others' goods, stealing, robbery, is what is meant. Herein, "what is not given" is another's possession, which the other may use as he likes without incurring penalty or blame. "Taking what is not given" is the volition to steal on the part of one who is aware, in respect of another's possession, that it is another's possession, and which (volition) initiates activity resulting in the taking of that thing.

That (taking of what is not given) is less blameworthy when the other's property is of low value, and more blameworthy when it is of high value. Why? Because of the high value of the object (stolen). When the value of the objects is equal, the act is more blameworthy when the object belongs to one of outstanding qualities, and less blameworthy when the object belongs to one who, in comparison, is inferior with respect to moral qualities.

There are five constituents of this act: another's possession, awareness that it is another's possession, the mind to steal, the activity, and the carrying off (of the object) thereby.

There are six means: one's own person, etc. (as for killing).

And these (acts of stealing) may be classed, according to the way in which they occur, by way of the following: taking by theft, by force, by concealment, by stratagem, by fraud. This here is in brief; the details, however, are given in the *Samantapāsādikā*.[9]

Misconduct in sensual pleasures (*kāmesu micchācāra*): here, "in sensual pleasures" (*kāmesu*) means in regard to sexual intercourse. "Misconduct" is entirely reprehensible vile conduct. As to characteristic, sexual misconduct is the volition to transgress bounds occurring through the body door by way of unrighteous intent.

Herein, out of bounds for men, firstly, are the twenty kinds of women, that is, the ten beginning with those protected by the mother, namely, "protected by the mother, protected by the father, protected by the mother and father, protected by the brother, protected by the sister, protected by relatives, protected by the clan, protected by the law, under protection, entailing a penalty"; and the ten beginning with those purchased with money, namely, "one purchased with money, one who lives (with a man) by her own desire, one who lives (with a man) on account of wealth, one who lives (with a man) on account of cloth, one who is given (in marriage with the ceremony of) dipping the hand in water, one who has been (taken to wife and) relieved of her burden-carrying head-pad, one who is a slave and a wife, one who is a servant and a wife, one who is carried off in a raid, one engaged at so much a time."[10]

Then, as concerns women, for the twelve kinds of women consisting of the two, namely, under protection and entailing a penalty, and the ten beginning with those purchased with money, other men are out of bounds.

This sexual misconduct is less blameworthy when (the person) out of bounds is without good qualities such as virtue, etc., and more blamewothy when (the person) possesses good qualities such as virtue, etc. There are four constituents of this act: an object which is out of bounds, the mind to engage in that, the effort to engage, and consent to the union of sexual organs.[11] The means is single: one's own person.

False speech (*musāvāda*): "false" (*musā*) is the verbal effort or bodily effort for destroying welfare (made) by one bent on deceiving. "False speech" is the volition initiating the verbal effort or bodily effort of deceiving another on the part of one intent on deceiving. According to another method, "false" means an unreal, untrue case, "speech" the communication of that as being real, true. As to characteristic, "false speech" is the volition of one desiring to communicate to another an untrue case as being true, which (volition) initiates such an act of communication.

This is less blameworthy when the welfare destroyed is slight, and more blameworthy when the welfare destroyed is great. Further, when it occurs on the part of householders who, not wishing to give away some belonging of theirs, say "I do not have it," it is less blameworthy; when one who is a witness speaks (falsely) for the purpose of destroying another's welfare, it is more blameworthy. In the case of those gone forth, when it occurs by their saying as a joke, after they have obtained just a little oil or ghee, in the manner of the Purāṇas, "Today the oil is flowing in the village just like a river," then it is less blameworthy; but for those who speak (as a witness) saying that they have seen what they have not seen it is more blameworthy.

There are four constituents of this act: an untrue case, the mind to deceive, the appropriate effort, the communicating of that meaning to another. The means is single: one's own person only. That is to be regarded as the performing of the action of deceiving another by means of the body or by means of something attached to the body or by means of speech. If, through that action, the other understands that meaning, one is bound by the kamma of false speech at the very moment of the volition initiating the action.

Malicious speech, etc.: The kind of speech that creates in the heart of the person to whom it is spoken affection for oneself and voidness (of affection) for another is malicious speech (*pisuṇā* *vācā*). The kind of speech by which one makes both oneself and another harsh, the kind of speech which is also itself harsh, being pleasant neither to the ear nor to the heart—that is **harsh speech** (*pharusā vācā*). That by which one gossips idly, without meaning, is **gossip** (*samphappalāpa*). Also, the volition that is the root cause of these gains the name "malicious speech," etc. And that only is intended here.

Therein, **malicious speech** is the volition of one with a defiled mind, which (volition) initiates an effort by body or by speech either to cause division among others or to endear oneself (to another). It is less blameworthy when the person divided has few good qualities, and more blameworthy when such a one has great qualities. Its constituents are four: another person to be divided, the intention to divide, (thinking) "Thus these will be separated and split" or the desire to endear oneself, (thinking) "Thus I shall become loved and intimate," the appropriate effort, the communicating of that meaning to that person.

Harsh speech is the entirely harsh volition initiating an effort by body or by speech to wound another's vital feelings. This is an example given for the purpose of making it clear: A village boy, it is said, went to the forest without heeding his mother's words. Unable to make him turn back, she scolded him angrily, saying: "May a wild buffalo chase you!" Then a buffalo appeared before him right there in the forest. The boy made an asseveration of truth, saying: "Let it not be as my mother said but as she thought!" The buffalo stood as though tied there. Thus, although the means (employed) was that of wounding the vital feelings, because of the gentleness of her mind it was not harsh speech. For sometimes parents even say to their children, "May robbers chop you to pieces!" yet they do not even wish a lotus leaf to fall upon them. And teachers and preceptors sometimes say to their pupils, "What is the use of these shameless and heedless brats? Drive them out!" yet they wish for their success in learning and attainment.

Just as, through gentleness of mind, speech is not harsh, so through gentleness of speech, speech does not become unharsh; for the words "Let him sleep in peace" spoken by one wishing to kill are not unharsh speech. But harsh speech is such on account of harshness of mind only. It is less blameworthy when the person to whom it is spoken has few good qualities, and more blameworthy when such a one has great qualities. Its constituents are three: another to be abused, an angry mind, the abusing.

Gossip is the unwholesome volition initiating an effort by body or by speech to communicate what is purposeless. It is less blameworthy when indulged in mildly, and more blameworthy when indulged in strongly. Its constituents are two: the being intent on purposeless stories such as the Bhārata war or the abduction of Sītā, etc., and the telling of such stories.[12]

Covetousness (*abhijjhā*): It covets, thus it is covetousness; "having become directed towards others' goods, it occurs through inclination towards them" is the meaning. It has the characteristic of coveting others' goods thus: "Oh, that this were mine!" It is less blameworthy and more blameworthy as in the case of taking what is not given. Its constituents are two: another's goods, and the inclination for them to be one's own. For even though greed has arisen based on another's goods, it is not classed as a (completed) course of kamma so long as one does not incline to them as one's own (with the thought), "Oh, that this were mine!"

Ill will (*byāpāda*): It injures welfare and happiness, thus it is ill will (*hitasukhaṁ byāpādayatī ti byāpādo*). Its characteristic is the mental defect (of wishing for) the destruction of others. It is less blameworthy and more blameworthy as in the case of harsh speech. Its constituents are two: another being, and the wish for that being's destruction. For even though anger has arisen based on another being, there is no breach of a course of kamma so long as one does not wish, "Oh, that this being might be cut off and destroyed!"

Wrong view (*micchādiṭṭhi*): It sees wrongly due to the absence of a correct grasp of things, thus it is wrong view. Its characteristic is the mistaken view that "there is no (result from) giving," etc. It is less blameworthy and more blameworthy as in the case of gossip. Moreover, it is less blameworthy when not fixed in destiny, and more blameworthy when fixed.[13] Its constituents are two: a mistaken manner of grasping the basis (for the view), and the appearance of that (basis) in accordance with the manner in which it has been grasped.

Now the exposition of these ten courses of unwholesome kamma should be understood in five ways: as to mental state (*dhammato*), as to category (*koṭṭhāsato*), as to object (*ārammaṇato*), as to feeling (*vedanāto*), and as to root (*mūlato*).

Herein, **as to mental state**: The first seven among these are volitional states only. The three beginning with covetousness are associated with volition.[14]

As to category: The eight consisting of the first seven and wrong view are courses of kamma only, not roots. Covetousness and ill will are courses of kamma and also roots; for covetousness, having arrived at the (state of) a root, is the unwholesome root greed, and ill will is the unwholesome root hate.

As to object: Killing living beings, because it has the life faculty as object, has a formation as object. Taking what is not given has beings as object or formations as object. Misconduct in sensual pleasures has formations as object by way of tangible object; but some say it also has beings as object. False speech has beings or formations as object; likewise malicious speech. Harsh speech has only beings as object. Gossip has either beings or formations as object by way of the seen, heard, sensed and cognized; likewise covetousness. Ill will has only beings as object. Wrong view has formations as object by way of the states belonging to the three planes (of being).

As to feeling: Killing living beings has painful feeling; for although kings, seeing a robber, say laughingly, "Go and execute him," their volition consummating the action is associated only with pain. Taking what is not given has three feelings. Misconduct (in sensual pleasures) has two feelings, pleasant and neutral, but in the mind which consummates the action there is no neutral feeling. False speech has three feelings; likewise malicious speech. Harsh speech has painful feeling only. Gossip has three feelings. Covetousness has two feelings, pleasant and neutral; likewise wrong view. Ill will has painful feeling only.

As to root: Killing living beings has two roots, by way of hate and delusion; taking what is not given, by way of hate and delusion or by way of greed and delusion; misconduct, by way of greed and delusion; false speech, by way of hate and delusion or by way of greed and delusion; likewise for malicious speech and gossip; harsh speech, by way of hate and delusion. Covetousness has one root, by way of delusion; likewise ill will. Wrong view has two roots, by way of greed and delusion.

The Unwholesome Roots

5. **Greed is a root of the unwholesome**, etc.: It is greedy, thus it is **greed** (*lubbhatī ti lobho*); it offends against (it hates), thus it is **hate** (*dussatī ti doso*); it deludes, thus it is **delusion** (*muyhatī ti moho*). Among these, greed is itself unwholesome in the sense that it is blameworthy and has painful results; and it is a root of these unwholesome (deeds) beginning with killing living beings, for some in the sense that it is an associated originative cause, for some in the sense that it is a decisive support condition. Thus it is an unwholesome root. This too is said: "One who is lustful, friends, overwhelmed and with mind obsessed by lust, kills a living being" (A.3:71/i,216; text slightly different). The same method applies to the state of being unwholesome roots in the cases of hate and delusion.

The Wholesome Courses of Action

6. **Abstention from killing living beings is wholesome** (*pāṇātipātā veramaṇī*), etc.: Here "killing living beings," etc. have the same meaning as aforesaid. It crushes the hostile, thus it is abstention (*veraṁ maṇatī ti veramaṇī*); the meaning is that it abandons the hostile. Or: with that as the instrument one abstains (*viramati*), the syllable *ve* being substituted for the syllable *vi*. This here is, in the first place, the commentary on the phrasing.

But as to the meaning, abstention is refraining (*virati*) associated with wholesome consciousness. What is stated thus: "For one refraining from killing living beings, that which is on that occasion the leaving off, the refraining" (Vibh. 285), that is the refraining associated with wholesome consciousness. As to kind, it is threefold: refraining in the presence of opportunity, refraining because of an undertaking, and refraining because of eradication (of defilements).

Herein, refraining in the presence of an opportunity (*sampattavirati*) is to be understood as the refraining which occurs in those who have not undertaken any training rule but who do not transgress when an opportunity for doing so presents itself because they reflect upon their birth, age, learning, etc., like the lay follower Cakkana in the island of Sri Lanka.

When he was a boy, it is said, his mother developed an illness, and the doctor said, "Fresh hare's flesh is needed." Then Cakkana's brother sent him, saying, "Go, dear, and hunt in the field." He went there. On that occasion a hare had come to eat the young corn. On seeing him it bolted swiftly, but it got entangled in a creeper and squealed "kiri, kiri." Guided by the sound, Cakkana went and caught it, thinking, "I will make medicine for my mother." Then he thought again, "This is not proper for me, that I should deprive another of life for the sake of my mother's life." So he released it, saying "Go and enjoy the grass and the water with the other hares in the forest." When his brother asked him, "Did you get a hare, dear?" he told him what had happened. His brother scolded him. He went to his mother and determined upon an asseveration of truth: "Since I was born I am not aware that I have ever intentionally deprived a living being of life." Straightaway his mother became well.

Refraining because of an undertaking (*samādānavirati*) is to be understood as the refraining which occurs in those who do not transgress in a particular case because they have undertaken training rules, giving up even their own lives in the undertaking of the training rules and in what is superior to that, like the lay follower who dwelt at Uttaravaddhamāna Mountain.

It is said that after undertaking the training rules from the Elder Pingala Buddharakkhita who lived in the Ambariya Monastery, he was ploughing a field. Then his ox got lost. Searching for it, he climbed up Uttaravaddhamāna Mountain. There a large serpent seized him. He thought, "Let me cut off his head with this sharp axe." Then he thought again, "This is not proper for me, that I should break a training rule that I have undertaken in the presence of my honoured teacher." Thinking up to the third time, "I will give up my life but not the training rule," he threw the sharp hand axe that was slung on his shoulder into the forest. Straightaway the creature released him and went away.

Refraining because of eradication (of defilements) (*samucchedavirati*) is to be understood as the refraining associated with the noble path. After the arising of this even the thought, "I will kill a living being," does not occur to the noble persons.

This refraining is called "wholesome" (*kusala*) because of the occurrence of wholesomeness (*kosalla*); or because of shedding the vile (*kucchitassa salanato*). Also, evil conduct is commonly called "weeds" (*kusa*) and it mows this down (*lunāti*), thus it is called "wholesome."

As in the case of the unwholesome, so for these courses of wholesome kamma the exposition should be understood in five ways: as to mental state, as to category, as to object, as to feeling, and as to root.

Herein, **as to mental state**: The first seven among these can be both volitions and abstinences; the last three are associated with volition only.

As to category: The first seven are courses of kamma only, not roots. The last three are courses of kamma and also roots. For non-covetousness, having arrived at the (state of) a root, is the wholesome root non-greed; non-ill will is the wholesome root non-hate; and right view is the wholesome root non-delusion.

As to object: The objects of these are the same as the objects of killing living beings, etc. For abstention is spoken of in relation to something which can be transgressed. But just as the noble path, which has Nibbāna as object, abandons the defilements, so too should these courses of kamma, which have the life faculty, etc., as object, be understood to abandon the kinds of evil conduct beginning with killing living beings.

As to feeling: All have pleasant feeling or neutral feeling. For there is no painful feeling which arrives at the wholesome.

As to root: The first seven courses of kamma have three roots by way of non-greed, non-hate, and non-delusion in one who abstains by means of consciousness associated with knowledge. They have two roots in one who abstains by means of consciousness dissociated from knowledge.[15] Non-covetousness has two roots in one who abstains by means of consciousness associated with knowledge, one root (in one who abstains) by means of consciousness dissociated from knowledge. Non-greed, however, is not by itself its own root. The same method applies in the case of non-ill will. Right view always has two roots, by way of non-greed and non-hate.[16]

The Wholesome Roots

7. **Non-greed is a root of the wholesome** (*alobho kusalamūlaṁ*), etc.: **Non-greed** is not greed; this is a term for the state that is opposed to greed. The same method applies in

the case of non-hate and non-delusion. Among these, non-greed is itself wholesome; and it is a root of these wholesome (courses of kamma) beginning with abstention from killing living beings, for some in the sense that it is an associated originative cause and for some in the sense that it is a decisive support condition. Thus it is a wholesome root. The same method applies to the state of being wholesome roots in the cases of non-hate and non-delusion.

Conclusion on the Unwholesome and the Wholesome

8. Now, summing up the meaning of all that has been set forth in brief and in detail, he states the concluding section beginning with the words **when a noble disciple**. Herein, **has thus understood the wholesome** (*evaṁ akusalaṁ pajānāti*) means: has thus understood the unwholesome by way of the ten courses of unwholesome kamma as described. The same method applies in the case of the root of the unwholesome, etc.

Up to this point, by a single method, emancipation as far as Arahantship has been expounded for one who has the Four Noble Truths as his meditation subject. How? Here, the ten courses of unwholesome kamma with the exception of covetousness, and the (ten) courses of wholesome kamma, are the truth of suffering. These two states—covetousness and the greed which is a root of the unwholesome—are, literally speaking, the truth of the origin. Speaking figuratively, however, all the courses of kamma are the truth of suffering, and all the wholesome and unwholesome roots are the truth of the origin.[17] The non-occurrence of both is the truth of cessation. The noble path fully understanding suffering, abandoning its origin, and understanding its cessation is the truth of the path. Thus two truths are stated in their own nature and two are to be understood by way of the guideline of conversion.[18]

He entirely abandons the underlying tendency to lust (*so sabbaso rāgānusayaṁ pahāya*): Understanding thus the unwholesome, etc., he abandons in all ways the underlying tendency to lust. **He abolishes the underlying tendency to aversion** (*paṭighānusayaṁ paṭivinodetvā*): and he removes in all ways too the underlying tendency to aversion, is what is meant. Up to this point the path of non-return is stated.[19] **He extirpates the underlying tendency to the view and conceit "I am"** (*asmī ti diṭṭhimānānusayaṁ samūhanitvā*): he extricates the underlying tendency to the view and conceit which occurs in the mode of grasping the five aggregates as a group (with the notion) "I am," due to failure to distinguish any state among them.

Therein, by the phrase **the underlying tendency to the view and conceit "I am"** (*diṭṭhimānānusayaṁ*) what is meant is the underlying tendency to conceit which is similar to a view (*diṭṭhisadisaṁ mānānusayaṁ*). For this underlying tendency to conceit is similar to a view because it occurs (with the notion) "I am"; therefore it is stated thus. And one who wishes to understand this conceit "I am" in detail should look up the Khemaka Sutta in the Khandhiyavagga (S.22:89/iii,126ff.).

By abandoning ignorance (*avijjaṁ pahāya*): having abandoned ignorance, the root of the round (of existence). **And arousing true knowledge** (*vijjaṁ uppādetvā*): having aroused the true knowledge of the path of Arahantship which completely extricates that ignorance. At this point the path of Arahantship is stated.[20] **He here and now makes an end of suffering** (*diṭṭh'eva dhamme dukkhass'antakaro hoti*): in this very existence he becomes one who cuts off the suffering of the round.

In that way too (*ettāvatāpi kho āvuso*): he marks off (this first part of) the teaching; by way of the attention and penetration stated in this exposition of the courses of kamma, is what is meant. The rest is as aforesaid. Thus he concludes the exposition by means of the path of non-return and the path of Arahantship.

The Four Nutriments

General

9. **Saying, "Good, friend," ... (etc.) ..." and has arrived at this true Dhamma"**: Thus, having heard the Venerable Sāriputta's exposition of the four truths under the heading of the wholesome and the unwholesome, the bhikkhus delighted in his words with the statement, "Good, friend," and rejoiced with the mind that aroused that statement; what is meant is that they agreed by word and approved by mind. Now, because the Elder was competent to give an exposition on the four truths in diverse ways—as (the Blessed One) said: "Bhikkhus, Sāriputta is able to propound, to teach, the Four Noble Truths in detail" (M.141/iii, 248); or because he had said "in that way too," being desirous of giving a further exposition, the bhikkhus, being desirous of hearing the teaching of the four truths by another method, asked him a further question. By asking "But, friend, might there be another way? Would there be another case?" they asked another question additional to that question asked and answered (already) by the Venerable Sāriputta himself. Or what is meant is that they asked a question subsequent to the previous one. Then, answering them, the Elder said, "There might be, friends," and so on.

10. Herein, this is the elucidation of the terms that are not clear. **Nutriment** (*āhāra*) is a condition (*paccaya*). For a condition nourishes its own fruit, therefore it is called nutriment.[21]

11. **Of beings that already have come to be** (*bhūtānaṁ vā sattānaṁ*), etc.: Here **come to be** (*bhūtā*) means come to birth, reborn; **seeking a new existence** (*sambhavesīnaṁ*) means those who seek, search for, existence, birth, production. Therein, among the four kinds of generation,[22] beings born from eggs and from the womb are said to be "seeking a new existence" as long as they have not broken out of the eggshell or the placenta. When they have broken out of the eggshell or the placenta and emerged

outside, they are said to have "come to be." The moisture-born and the spontaneously born are said to be "seeking a new existence" at the first moment of consciousness; from the second moment of consciousness onwards they are said to have "come to be."

Or alternatively, "come to be" is born, reproduced; this is a term for those who have destroyed the cankers (Arahants), who are reckoned thus: "They have come to be only, but they will not come to be again." "Seeking a new existence" means they seek a new existence; this is a term for worldlings and disciples in higher training who seek a new existence in the future too, because they have not abandoned the fetter of being. Thus by these two terms he includes all beings in all ways.

For the maintenance (*ṭhitiyā*); for the purpose of maintaining. **For the support** (*anuggahāya*): for the purpose of supporting, for the purpose of helping. This is merely a difference of words, but the meaning of the two terms is one only. Or alternatively, "for the maintenance" is for the non-interruption of this or that being by means of the serial connection of arisen states. "For the support" is for the arising of unarisen (states). And both these expressions should be regarded as applicable in both cases thus: "For the maintenance and support of those that have come to be, and for the maintenance and support of those seeking a new existence."

The Four Kinds of Nutriment

Physical food as nutriment (lit. "food made into a ball") (*kabaḷinkāro āhāro*) is nutriment that can be swallowed after making it into a ball; this is a term for the nutritive essence which has as its basis boiled rice, junket, etc.[23] **Gross or subtle** (*oḷāriko vā sukhumo vā*): it is gross because of the grossness of the basis, and subtle because of the subtlety of the basis. But because physical nutriment is included in subtle materiality, by way of its individual essence it is subtle only.[24] And also that grossness and subtlety should be understood relatively in respect of the basis.

The nutriment of peacocks is subtle compared with the nutriment of crocodiles. Crocodiles, they say, swallow stones, and these dissolve on reaching their stomachs. Peacocks eat such animals as snakes, scorpions, etc. But the nutriment of hyenas is subtle compared with the nutriment of peacocks. These, they say, eat horns and bones thrown away three years before, and these become soft as yams as soon as they are moistened with their saliva. Also, the nutriment of elephants is subtle compared with the nutriment of hyenas. For these eat the branches of various trees, etc. The nutriment of the gayal buffalo, the antelope, the deer, etc., is subtler than the nutriment of elephants. These, they say, eat the sapless leaves of various kinds of trees, etc. The nutriment of cows is subtler than their nutriment; they eat fresh and dried grass. The nutriment of hares is subtler than their nutriment; that of birds is subtler than that of hares; that of barbarians is subtler than that of birds; that of village headmen is subtler than that of barbarians; that of kings and kings' ministers is subtler than village headmens'; that of a Wheel-turning Monarch is subtler than their nutriment. The earth deities' nutriment is subtler than that of a Wheel-turning Monarch. The nutriment of the deities of the Four Great Kings is subtler than that of the earth deities. Thus nutriment should be elaborated up to that of the deities who wield power over others' creations.[25] But saying, "Their nutriment is subtle," the end is reached.

And here, in a basis that is gross, the nutritive essence is limited and weak; in one that is subtle, it is strong. Thus one who has drunk even a full bowl of gruel is soon hungry again and desirous of eating anything; but after drinking even a small amount of ghee, he will not want to eat for the whole day. Therein, it is the basis that dispels fatigue, but it is unable to preserve; but the nutritive essence preserves, though it cannot dispel fatigue. But when the two are combined they both dispel fatigue and preserve.

Contact as the second (*phasso dutiyo*): The sixfold contact beginning with eye-contact should be understood as the second of these four kinds of nutriment. And this is the method of the teaching itself; therefore it should not be inquired into here, saying "For this reason it is the second, or the third." **Mental volition** (*manosañcetanā*): volition (*cetanā*) itself is stated. **Consciousness** (*viññāṇaṁ*): any kind of consciousness whatever.

It may be asked here: "If the meaning of condition is the meaning of nutriment, then, when other conditions also exist for beings, why are only these four stated?" It should be said in reply: "It is because they are the special conditions for personal continuity." For physical nutriment is the special condition for the material body of beings that eat physical nutriment; as regards the group of mental constituents, contact is (the special condition) for feeling, mental volition for consciousness, and consciousness for mentality-materiality. As it is said: "Just as, bhikkhus, this body has nutriment for its maintenance, is maintained in dependence on nutriment, and without nutriment is not maintained" (S.46:2/v,64); and likewise: "With contact as condition, feeling; ... with formations as condition, consciousness; ... with consciousness as condition, mentality-materiality" (S.12:1/ii,1, etc.).

What is this nutriment, and what does it nourish? Physical nutriment nourishes the materiality with nutritive essence as eighth;[26] contact as nutriment nourishes the three feelings; mental volition as nutriment nourishes the three kinds of being; consciousness as nutriment nourishes the mentality-materiality of rebirth-linking.

How? As soon as it is placed in the mouth, physical food as nutriment brings into being the eight kinds of materiality (aforesaid). Then each lump of cooked rice ground by the teeth, on being swallowed, brings into being unit after unit of the eight kinds of materiality. Thus it nourishes the materiality with nutritive essence as eighth.

But with contact as nutriment, when contact productive of pleasant feeling arises it nourishes pleasant feeling; contact productive of painful feeling nourishes painful feeling; contact productive of neither-painful-nor-pleasant feeling nourishes neither-painful-nor-pleasant feeling. Thus in all ways contact as nutriment nourishes the three kinds of feeling.

In the case of mental volition as nutriment, kamma leading to sense-sphere being nourishes sense-sphere being; kamma leading to fine-material and immaterial being nourishes its respective kind of being. Thus in all ways mental volition as nutriment nourishes the three kinds of being.

But with consciousness as nutriment, it is said that it nourishes, by way of conascence condition, etc., the three (immaterial) aggregates associated with itself at the moment of rebirth-linking and the thirty kinds of materiality that arise by way of triple continuity. Thus consciousness nourishes the mentality-materiality of rebirth-linking.[27]

And here, by the words "mental volition as nutriment nourishes the three kinds of being," only the wholesome and unwholesome volition accompanied by taints is meant; by the words "consciousness nourishes the mentality-materiality of rebirth-linking," only rebirth-linking consciousness is meant. However, these are to be understood indiscriminately as nutriments as well because they nourish the states that are associated with them and originated by them.

The Four Functions

As regards these four kinds of nutriment, physical food as nutriment accomplishes the function of nutriment by sustaining, contact by contacting (touching), mental volition by accumulating, consciousness by cognizing.

How? Physical food as nutriment, by sustaining, is for the

maintenance of beings by maintaining the body. For this body, though generated by kamma, is sustained by physical food and stands for ten years or a hundred years up to the end of the life-span. Like what? Like a child which, though given birth by the mother, is nurtured by the milk, etc., given to him to drink by the wet-nurse and thus lives long. Also, as a house is supported by a prop. This too has been said (untraced): "Great king, just as, when a house is collapsing, they prop it up with other timber, and that house, being propped up by other timber, does not collapse, so too this body is supported by nutriment, persists in dependence upon nutriment."

Thus physical food as nutriment accomplishes the function of nutriment by sustaining. Accomplishing it thus, physical food as nutriment becomes a condition for two material continuities, namely, for that originated by nutriment and that kammically acquired.[28] It is a condition for the kamma-born materiality by becoming its preserver. It is a condition for that originated by nutriment by becoming its producer.

Then contact, by contacting the object which is the basis for pleasure, etc., is "for the maintenance of beings" by causing the occurrence of pleasant feeling, etc. Mental volition, accumulating by way of wholesome and unwholesome kamma, is "for the maintenance of beings" because it provides the root of existence. Consciousness, by cognizing, is "for the maintenance of beings" by causing the occurrence of mentality-materiality.

The Four Dangers

Now, while these are accomplishing their function of nutriment by sustaining, etc., four dangers are to be seen: the danger of desire in the case of physical food as nutriment; the danger of approach in the case of contact; (the danger) of accumulating in the case of mental volition; and (the danger) of launching [into a new existence here or there by way of taking rebirth-linking] in the case of consciousness.

What are the reasons (for this)? Because, having aroused desire for physical food, beings face cold, etc., to undertake such work as checking, accounting, etc., and incur not a little suffering. And some who have gone forth in this dispensation seek nutriment through such improper means as the practice of medicine, etc., and they are to be censured here and now, and hereafter they become "recluse ghosts" in the manner described thus in the Lakkhaṇa Saṁyutta: "And his outer robe was burning, blazing," etc.[29] For this reason, desire itself is to be understood as the danger in physical food as nutriment.

Those who approach contact, who find gratification in contact, commit crimes in respect of others' guarded and protected belongings, such as their wives, etc. When the owners of the goods catch them with their belongings, they cut them into pieces or throw them onto a rubbish heap, or hand them over to the king; and then the king has various tortures inflicted upon them. And with the breakup of the body, after death, a bad destination is to be expected for them. Thus this entire danger—that pertaining to the here and now and that pertaining to the afterlife—has come about rooted in contact. For this reason, approach is to be understood as the danger in the case of the nutriment contact.

The entire danger in the three realms of existence has come about by the accumulation of wholesome and unwholesome kamma and is rooted in that (accumulation). For this reason, accumulation is to be understood as the danger in the nutriment mental volition.

And in whatever place rebirth-linking consciousness launches (the new existence), in that same place it is reborn by seizing the rebirth-linking mentality-materiality. When it is produced, all dangers are produced, for they are all rooted in it. For this reason, launching is to be understood as the danger in the nutriment consciousness.

The Four Similes

In regard to these nutriments with their dangers, for the sake of eliminating desire for the nutriment physical food, the Fully Enlightened One taught **the simile of son's flesh** in the passage beginning thus: "Suppose, bhikkhus, a couple, a man and his wife, ..." For the sake of eliminating desire for the nutriment contact, he taught **the simile of the flayed cow** in the passage beginning thus: "Suppose, bhikkhus, there was a flayed cow ..." For the sake of eliminating desire for the nutriment mental volition, he taught **the simile of the charcoal pit** in the passage beginning thus: "Suppose, bhikkhus, there was a charcoal pit ..." And for the sake of eliminating desire for the nutriment consciousness, he taught **the simile of the man struck with three hundred spears** in the passage beginning thus: "Suppose, bhikkhus, there was a thief, a crook ..."[30]

Therein, taking the essential meaning, there follows a brief interpretation of the meaning. A couple, it is said, a man and his wife, took their son and set out on a desert trail a hundred *yojanas* long,[31] with only limited provisions. When they had gone fifty *yojanas* their provisions ran out. Exhausted by hunger and thirst, they sat down in some scanty shade. Then the man said to his wife: "My dear, for fifty *yojanas* on all sides there is neither a village nor a town. Therefore, though a man can do many kinds of work, such as ploughing, guarding cattle, etc., it is not possible for me to do that. Come, kill me. Eat half of my flesh, and having made the other half into provisions for the journey, cross out of the desert together with our son."

The wife said: "Dear husband, though a woman can do many kinds of work, such as spinning thread, etc., it is not possible for me to do that. Come, kill me. Eat half of my flesh, and having made the other half into provisions for the journey, cross out of the desert together with our son."

Then the man said: "My dear, the death of the mother would mean the death of two, for a young boy cannot live without his mother. But if we both live, then we can beget another child again. Come now, let us kill our child, take his flesh, and cross out of this desert."

Then the mother said to the son: "Dear, go to your father." He went, but the father said: "For the sake of supporting this child I incurred much suffering through such work as ploughing, guarding cattle, etc. I cannot kill the boy. You kill your son." Then he said: "Dear, go to your mother." But the mother said: "Longing for a son I incurred much suffering by observing the cow-observance, the dog-observance, praying to the gods, etc., not to speak of bearing him in my womb.[32] It is not possible for me to kill him." Then she said: "Dear, go to your father."

The boy died from going back and forth between the father and the mother. Seeing him dead, they wept, and having taken the flesh as described above, they departed. Because that flesh of their son was repulsive to them for nine reasons, it was not eaten for enjoyment nor for intoxication nor for making (the body) strong and beautiful, but only for the purpose of crossing out of the desert.

For what nine reasons was it repulsive? Because it was the flesh of their own offspring, the flesh of a relative, the flesh of a son, the flesh of a dear son, the flesh of a youngster, raw flesh, not beef, unsalted, unspiced. Therefore the bhikkhu who sees the nutriment physical food thus, as similar to son's flesh, eliminates the desire for it.[33]

This, in the first place, is the interpretation of the meaning of **the simile of son's flesh**.

Then, as regards **the simile of the flayed cow**: If a cow were stripped of its skin from the neck to the hooves and then set free, whatever it would rest upon would become a basis of pain for it, since it would be bitten by the small creatures living there.[34] So too, whatever physical basis or object contact stands upon as its support becomes a basis for the felt pain originating from that basis or object.[35] Therefore a bhikkhu who sees the nutriment contact thus, as similar to a flayed cow, eliminates the desire for it. This is the interpretation of the meaning of the simile of the flayed cow.

Then, as regards **the simile of the charcoal pit:**[36] The three realms of being are like a charcoal pit in the sense of a great burning heat (lit., a great fever). Like the two men who grab hold (of a weaker man) by both his arms and drag him towards it, is mental volition in the sense that it drags one towards the realms of being. Therefore a bhikkhu who sees the nutriment mental volition thus, as similar to a charcoal pit, eliminates the desire for it. This is the interpretation of the meaning of the simile of the charcoal pit.

Then, as regards **the simile of the man struck with three hundred spears:**[37] The hundred spears that strike the man in the morning make a hundred wound openings in his body, and without remaining inside they pierce through and fall on the other side; and so with the other two hundred spears as well. Thus his whole body is cut again and again by the spears which come without piercing him in a place where another has already struck. There is no measuring the pain arisen in him from even one of the wound openings, not to speak of three hundred wound openings.

Therein, the time of the generation of the rebirth-linking consciousness is like the time of being struck by a spear. The production of the aggregates is like the production of the wound openings. The arising of the various kinds of suffering rooted in the round (of existence) once the aggregates have been born is like the arising of suffering on account of the wound openings.

Another method of interpretation (is as follows): The rebirth-linking consciousness is like the thief. His mentality-materiality conditioned by consciousness is like the wound openings created by the striking of the spears. The arising of the various kinds of suffering by way of the thirty-two types of torture and the eighty-nine types of diseases in regard to consciousness conditioned by mentality-materiality—this should be regarded as like the arising of severe pain for that man conditioned by the wound openings.

Therefore a bhikkhu who sees the nutriment consciousness thus, as similar to one struck by three hundred spears, eliminates the desire for it. This is the interpretation of the meaning of the simile of the man struck by three hundred spears.

Full Understanding

Thus by eliminating desire in regard to these nutriments, he also fully understands these four nutriments. When these have been fully understood, the entire basis (for them) has also been fully understood. For this has been said by the Blessed One (S.12:63/ii,99-100):

> Bhikkhus, when the nutriment physical food has been fully understood, lust for the five cords of sensual pleasure has been fully understood. When lust for the five cords of sensual pleasure has been fully understood, there exists no more any fetter bound by which the noble disciple might come back to this world.
>
> Bhikkhus, when the nutriment contact has been fully understood, the three feelings have been fully understood. When the three feelings have been fully understood, there is nothing further for the noble disciple to do, I say.
>
> Bhikkhus, when the nutriment mental volition has been fully understood, the three kinds of craving have been fully understood. When the three kinds of craving have been fully understood, there is nothing further for the noble disciple to do, I say.
>
> Bhikkhus, when the nutriment consciousness has been fully understood, mentality-materiality has been fully understood. When mentality-materiality has been fully understood, there is nothing further for the noble disciple to do, I say.

The Arising and Cessation of Nutriment

With the arising of craving there is the arising of nutriment (*taṇhāsamudayā āhārasamudayo*): This is the meaning: "With the arising of craving in the previous (existence) the arising of the nutriments occurs at rebirth-linking (in this existence)." How? Because at the moment of rebirth-linking there is the nutritive essence produced among the thirty types of materiality that have arisen by way of triple continuity.[38] This is the kammically acquired physical food as nutriment produced by craving as its condition. But the contact and volition associated with the rebirth-linking consciousness, and that mind or consciousness itself—these are the kammically acquired nutriments of contact, mental volition and consciousness produced by craving as their condition. Thus, in the first place, the arising of the nutriments at rebirth-linking should be understood as occurring with the arising of craving in the previous existence.

But because the nutriments that are kammically acquired and those that are not kammically acquired have been discussed here combined, (the principle of) the arising of nutriment with the arising of craving should be understood to apply also to those that are not kammically acquired. For there is nutritive essence in the kinds of materiality that are aroused by the eight types of consciousness accompanied by greed;[39] this is the nutriment physical food that is not kammically acquired yet is produced by conascent craving as its condition. But the contact and volition associated with the consciousness accompanied by greed, and that mind or consciousness itself—these are the nutriments of contact, mental volition and consciousness that are not kammically acquired yet are produced by craving as their condition.

With the cessation of craving there is cessation of nutriment (*taṇhānirodhā āhāranirodho*): By this there is set forth the cessation of nutriment by the cessation of the craving that had become the condition for both nutriment that is kammically acquired and that which is not kammically acquired. The rest (should be understood) by the method stated, but there is this difference. Here the four truths are stated directly, and as here, so in all the following sections. Therefore one who is unconfused in mind can deduce the truths throughout in what follows.[40]

12. And in all the following sections the delimiting phrase **In that way too, friends** (*ettāvatā pi kho āvuso*) should be construed according to the principle that has been expounded. Here, in the first place, this is the interpretation of it (in the present context). "In that way too": what is meant is: "the attention and penetration stated by way of the teaching concerning nutriment." The same method throughout.

The Four Noble Truths

14. Now, delighting and rejoicing in the Elder's words, after saying as before "Good, friend," the bhikkhus asked a further question, and the Elder answered them by another exposition. This method is found in all the following sections. Therefore, from here onwards, we shall explain the meaning only of the particular exposition he states in reply, without touching upon such words (as are already explained).

15. In the brief exposition of this teaching, in the phrase **(he) understands suffering** (*dukkhaṁ pajānāti*), "suffering" is the truth of suffering. But regarding the detailed exposition, whatever needs to be said has all been said already in the *Visuddhimagga* in the Description of the Truths (XVI,13-104).

Ageing and Death

21. From here onwards the teaching is given by way of dependent arising (*paṭicca samuppāda*).

22. Therein, in the section on ageing and death, firstly as to the term **their** (*tesaṁ tesaṁ*)—this should be understood as a collective designation in brief for the many kinds of beings. For if one were to state (the ageing of individuals such as) the age-

ing of Devadatta, the ageing of Somadatta, etc., one would never come to an end of beings. But there is no being not included by this term "their."[41] Therefore it was said above: "This should be understood as a collective designation in brief for the many kinds of beings."

In the various (*tamhi tamhi*): This is a collective designation for the many (different) orders by way of destiny and birth. **Orders of beings** (*sattanikaye*): an indication of the nature of what is designated by the collective designation.

Ageing, old age (*jarā jīraṇatā*), etc.: As regards these, "ageing" is the description of the nature; "old age" is the description of the aspect; "brokenness," etc., are descriptions of the function with respect to the passage of time; and the last two terms are descriptions of the normal (process). For this is indicated as to nature by this term **ageing** (*jarā*); hence this is a description of its nature. It is indicated as to aspect by this term **old age** (*jīraṇatā*); hence this is a description of its aspect. **Brokenness** (*khaṇḍicca*): by this it is indicated as to the function of causing the broken state of teeth and nails on account of the passage of time. **Greyness** (*pālicca*): by this it is indicated as to the function of causing the head hairs and body hairs to turn grey. **Wrinkling** (*valittacatā*): by this it is indicated as to the wrinkled state of the skin after the withering of the flesh. Hence the three terms beginning with brokenness are descriptions of function with respect to the passage of time. By these evident ageing is shown, which becomes evident by the showing of these alterations. For just as the course taken by water or wind or fire is evident from the damaged and broken state, or the burnt state, of the grass and trees, etc., and yet the course that has been taken is not the water, etc., itself, so too the course taken by ageing is evident through brokenness of teeth, etc., and it is apprehended by opening the eyes, but the brokenness, etc., themselves are not ageing, nor is ageing cognizable by the eye.

Decline of life, weakness of faculties (*āyuno samhāni*

indriyānaṁ paripāko): By these terms it is indicated by means of the normal (process) known as the exhaustion of the life-span and the weakening of the eye faculty, etc., that has become manifest with the passage of time. Hence these last two are to be understood as descriptions of its normal (process).

Therein, because the life-span of one who has reached ageing is dwindling, ageing is called "decline of life" as a metaphor (for the cause stated in terms) of its effect. And because the eye faculty, etc.—which at the time of youth were quite clear and could easily grasp even subtle objects—become deficient, obscure, unable to grasp even gross objects when one has reached old age, therefore it is called "weakness of faculties" also as a metaphor (for the cause stated in terms) of its effect.

This ageing, thus described, is all of two kinds, evident and concealed. Therein, the ageing of material phenomena, shown by brokenness, etc., is called **evident ageing** (*pākaṭajarā*). But in the case of immaterial phenomena, because their alteration in such a way is not visible, their ageing is called **concealed ageing** (*paṭicchannajarā*). Therein, the brokenness that is seen is simply colour (*vaṇṇa*) because of the ease of comprehending such things as the teeth, etc. Having seen this with the eye and reflected on it with the mind door, one knows ageing thus: "These teeth have been afflicted by ageing," just as one knows the existence of water below when one has noticed the heads of cows, etc., bound to the place where the water is located.

Again, ageing is twofold thus: as continuous and as discrete. Therein, **continuous ageing** (*avīcijarā*) is the ageing of such things as gems, gold, silver, coral, the sun and moon, etc.; it is so called because of the difficulty of perceiving in such things distinct changes in colour, etc., at regular intervals, as we can in the case of living beings passing through the decade of childhood, etc., and in the case of vegetation (lit. non-breathing things) such as flowers, fruits, buds, etc. The meaning is: ageing that progresses without interval. **Discrete ageing** (*savīcijarā*) is the ageing of the things other than those, i.e. of the aforesaid things (living beings and vegetation); it is so called because it is easy to perceive in them distinct changes in colour, etc., at regular intervals. So it should be understood.

Following this (in the definition of death) the term **their** (*tesaṁ tesaṁ*) should be understood by the method stated above (in the definition of ageing). Then, in the expression **passing, passing away**, etc., **passing** (*cuti*) is said by way of what has the nature to pass away; this is a collective designation (applying) to one-, four-, and five-aggregate (existence). **Passing away** (*cavanatā*) is the indication of the characteristic by a word expressing the abstract state. **Dissolution** (*bheda*) is an indication of the occurrence of the breaking up of the aggregates (at the time) of passing. **Disappearance** (*antaradhāna*) is an indication of the absence of any manner of persistence of the aggregates (at the time) of passing, as they are broken like a broken pot.

Dying (*maccu maraṇa*): death which is called dying. By this he rejects the idea of death as complete annihilation. **Completion of time** (*kālakiriyā*): time is the destroyer, and this (completion of time) is its activity. By this he explains death in conventional terminology.

Now, to explain death in (terms valid in) the ultimate sense, he next says **the dissolution of the aggregates** (*khandhānaṁ bhedo*), etc.[42] For in the ultimate sense it is only the aggregates that break up; it is not any so called being that dies. But when the aggregates are breaking up convention says "a being is dying," and when they have broken up convention says "(he is) dead."

Here the dissolution of the aggregates is said by way of four-[and five-] constituent being; the laying down of the body (*kaḷevarassa nikkhepo*) by way of one-constituent being.[43] Or alternatively, the dissolution of the aggregates is said by way of four-constituent being; the laying down of the body should be understood by way of the other two (i.e. one- and five-constituent being). Why? Because of the existence of the body, that is, the material body, in those two realms of being. Or else, because in the realm of the Four Great Kings, etc., the aggregates simply break up and they do not lay anything down, the dissolution of the aggregates is said with reference to them.[44] The laying down of the body occurs among human beings, etc. And here, because it is the cause for the laying down of the body, death is called the laying down of the body. Thus the meaning should be understood.

So this ageing and this death are what is called ageing and death (*iti ayañ ca jarā idañ ca maraṇaṁ idaṁ vuccat'āvuso jarāmaraṇaṁ*): this is spoken of as "ageing and death" by combining the two into one.

Birth

26. In the section on birth, in regard to the phrase **birth, ... their coming to birth**, etc., **birth** (*jāti*) is in the sense of being born; this is stated with reference to those (conceived) with incomplete sense bases. **Coming to birth** (*sañjāti*) is in the sense of the act of coming to birth; this is stated with reference to those (conceived) with already complete sense bases. **Precipitation** (or descent, *okkanti*) is in the sense of being precipitated (descending). This is stated with reference to those born from the egg and from the womb, for they take rebirth-linking as though descending and entering the egg shell or the placenta. **Generation** (*abhinibbatti*) is in the sense of being generated. This is stated with reference to those born from moisture or those of spontaneous birth, for these are generated as soon as they become manifest.

Now comes the exposition in (terms valid in) the ultimate sense. **Manifestation** (*pātubhāva*) is the arising. **Of the aggregates** (*khandhānaṁ*) is to be understood as (the arising) of one aggregate in the one-constituent realm of being, of four aggregates in four-constituent realms, and of five aggregates in five-constituent realms. **Obtaining** (*paṭilābha*) is the manifestation in continuity. **The bases** (*āyatanānaṁ*) should be understood as comprising the sense bases arising (at conception) in this or that realm. For when the sense bases become manifest, then they are said to be obtained.

This is called birth (*ayaṁ vuccat'āvuso jāti*): by this phrase he comes to the conclusion on birth taught in both conventional terms and in the ultimate sense.

With the arising of being (*bhavasamudayā*): but here one should understand kammically active being as the condition for birth. The rest by the method stated.

Being

30. In the section on being, **sense-sphere being** (*kāmabhava*) is kammically active being and resultant being. Therein, **kammically active being** (*kammabhava*) is kamma itself that leads to sense-sphere being. For that is called "being" as a designation of the cause in terms of its effect, because it is the cause for resultant being, as when it is said: "The arising of Buddhas is bliss" and "The accumulation of evil is painful" (Dhp. 194, 117). **Resultant being** (*upapattibhava*) is the group of kammically acquired aggregates produced by that kamma. For that is called "being" because it exists there. Thus this kamma and this result are both spoken of conjointly as "sense-sphere being." The same method applies to **fine-material being** and **immaterial being** (*rūpārūpabhava*).

With the arising of clinging (*upādānasamudayā*): But here clinging is a condition for wholesome kammically active being only by way of decisive support; it is a condition for unwholesome kammically active being by way of both decisive support and conascence.[45] For all resultant being it is a condition only by way of decisive support. The rest by the method stated.

Clinging

34. In the section on clinging, in regard to the phrase "clinging to sense pleasures," etc., **clinging to sense pleasures** (*kāmupādāna*) is analyzed thus: by this one clings to the object of sensual pleasure, or this itself clings to it. Or alternatively: that is a sensual pleasure and it is clinging, thus it is clinging to sensual pleasure. It is firm grasping (*daḷhagahaṇa*) that is called clinging. For here the prefix *upa* has the sense of firmness. This is a designation for the lust for the five cords of sensual pleasure. This is the brief account here. The detailed account should be understood by the method stated thus: "Therein, what is clinging to sensual pleasures? The sensual desire in regard to sensual pleasures," etc. (Dhs. §1214).

So too, that is a view and clinging, thus it is **clinging to views** (*diṭṭhupādāna*). Or alternatively: it clings to a view, or by this they cling to a view. For the subsequent view clings to the previous view and thereby they cling to the view. As it is said: "Self and the world are eternal; only this is true, anything else is false," etc. (M.102/ii, 233). This is a designation for the whole field of (wrong) views except clinging to rituals and observances and clinging to a doctrine of self.[46] This is the brief account here. The detailed account should be understood by the method stated thus: "Therein, what is clinging to views? There is nothing given," etc. (Dhs. §1215).

So too, by this they cling to rituals and observances, or this itself clings to them, or that is a ritual and observance and clinging, thus it is **clinging to rituals and observances** (*sīlabbatupādāna*). For when one adheres to the idea that the cow ritual or cow observance brings purification, that itself is a clinging.[47] This is the brief account here. The detailed account should be understood by the method stated thus: "Therein, what is clinging to rituals and observances? (The idea) of recluses and brahmins outside here (i.e. outside the Buddha's dispensation) that purity (is achieved) by rules," etc. (Dhs. §1216).

Now they assert in terms of this, thus it is a doctrine. By this they cling, thus it is clinging. What do they assert? Or what do they cling to? Self. The clinging to a doctrine about a self is the **clinging to a doctrine of self** (*attavādupādāna*). Or alternatively: by this a mere doctrine of self is clung to as self, thus it is clinging to a doctrine of self. This is a designation for personality view with its twenty cases. This is the brief account here. The detailed account should be understood by the method stated thus: "Therein, what is clinging to a doctrine of self? Here, the uninstructed worldling who has no regard for noble ones," etc. (Dhs. §1217).

With the arising of craving (*taṇhāsamudayā*): here, craving is a condition for clinging to sensual pleasures either by way of decisive support or by way of proximity, contiguity, absence, disappearance and repetition.[48] But for the rest (it is a condition) by way of conascence, etc., too. The rest by the method stated.

Craving

38. In the section on craving, **craving for forms ... craving for mind-objects** (*rūpataṇhā ... dhammataṇhā*): these are names for the kinds of craving which occur in the course of a javana cognitive process (*javanavīthi*) in the eye door, etc. Like a name derived from the father, such as Seṭṭhiputta ("merchant's son") or Brahmaṇaputta ("brahmin's son"), their names are derived from the object, which is similar to the father [as being the cause (*hetu*) of it only, not as is the case with "eye-contact," which is like a name derived from the mother in that (the eye like the mother in relation to her son) is a cause by its nature as a physical support (*nissayabhava*)].

And here, **craving for forms** is craving that has forms as its object, craving in regard to forms. When this occurs by finding gratification in visible forms through its nature as sensual lust, it is **craving for sensual pleasure** (*kāmataṇhā*). When it occurs by finding gratification in visible forms, thinking "Form is permanent, lasting, eternal," through its nature as lust accompanied by the eternalist view, then it is **craving for being** (*bhavataṇhā*). When it occurs by finding gratification in visible form, thinking "Form is annihilated, destroyed, and does not exist after death," through its nature as lust accompanied by the annihilationist view, then it is **craving for non-being** (*vibhavataṇhā*). Thus it is threefold. And as craving for form, so too craving for sound, etc., (are each threefold too). Thus there are eighteen modes of craving. These eighteen in respect of internal visible form, etc., and in respect of external visible form, etc., come to thirty-six. So thirty-six in the past, thirty-six in the future, and thirty-six at present make up a hundred and eight.

Or there are eighteen based on internal form, etc., thus: "On account of the internal there is (the notion) 'I am,' there is (the notion) 'I am such and such,' " and so on; and there are eighteen based on external form, etc., thus: "On account of the external there is (the notion) 'I am,' there is (the notion) 'I am such and such,' " and so on. Thus there are thirty-six. So thirty-six in the past, thirty-six in the future, and thirty-six at present make up thus the hundred and eight modes of craving (*taṇhāvicaritāni*; see A. 4:199/ii, 212).

Again, when a classification is made, they reduce to only six classes of craving—in terms of their objects, forms and the rest—and to only three types of craving—craving for sensual pleasure and the rest. Thus:

Craving should be known by the wise
Through description and when described
In detail; it (should be known) again
Through classification of the detail.

With the arising of feeling there is the arising of crav-

ing (*vedanāsamudayā taṇhasamudayo*): But here the word "feeling" is intended as resultant feeling.[49] How is that the condition for craving in respect of the six sense doors? Because of its ability to produce gratification. For it is through the gratification in pleasant feeling that beings become enamoured of that feeling, and after arousing craving for feeling and being seized by lust for feeling, they long only for a desirable visible form in the eye door. And on getting it, they find gratification in it, and they honour painters, etc., who provide such objects. Likewise, they long only for a desirable sound, etc., in the ear door, etc. And on getting it, they find gratification in it, and they honour musicians, perfume makers, cooks, spinners and the teachers of the various crafts. Like what? Like those who, being enamoured of a child, out of love for the child honour the wet-nurse and give her suitable ghee, milk, etc., to eat and drink. The rest by the method stated.

Feeling

42. In the section on feeling, **classes of feeling** (*vedanākāya*) means groups of feeling. **Feeling born of eye-contact ... feeling born of mind-contact** (*cakkhusamphassajā vedanā ... manosamphassajā vedanā*): because of what has come down in the *Vibhaṅga* thus: "There is feeling born of eye-contact that is wholesome, that is unwholesome, that is indeterminate" (Vibh. 15), the wholesome, unwholesome and indeterminate feelings that occur in the eye door, etc., are named after the physical base, which is similar to a mother, just as some are named after their mother, such as "Sāriputta (Lady Sāri's son)," "Mantāṇiputta (Lady Mantāṇi's son)," etc.

But the word meaning here is this: **feeling born of eye-contact** (*cakkhusamphassajā vedanā*) is feeling that is born with eye-contact as the cause. The same method throughout. This, in the first place, is the all-inclusive explanation. But by way of resultant, in the eye-door there are two eye-consciousnesses, two mind elements, three mind-consciousness elements; feeling should be understood as what is associated with these.[50] This method also applies in the ear door, etc. In the mind door, (feeling) is associated only with the mind-consciousness elements.

With the arising of contact (*phassasamudayā*): But here the arising in the five doors of the feelings that have the five physical bases (as their support) occurs with the arising of the conascent eye-contact. For the rest, eye-contact, etc., are conditions by way of decisive support. In the mind door, the arising of feelings (on the occasion) of registration and of the doorless feelings (on the occasions) of rebirth-linking, life-continuum and death occurs with the arising of the conascent mind-contact.[51] The rest by the method stated.

Contact

46. In the section on contact, **eye-contact** (*cakkhusamphassa*) is contact in the eye. The same method throughout. **Eye-contact ... body-contact** (*cakkhusamphasso ... kāyasamphasso*): up to this point ten kinds of contact have been stated, namely, the wholesome- and unwholesome-resultants having the five physical bases (as their support). **Mind-contact** (*manosamphassa*): by this (he indicates) the remaining twenty-two kinds of contact associated with the mundane resultant (types of consciousness).[52]

With the arising of the sixfold base (*saḷāyatanasamudayā*): The arising of this sixfold contact should be understood to occur by way of the arising of the six bases beginning with the eye-base. The rest by the method stated.

The Sixfold Base

50. In the section on the sixfold base, as regards **the eye-base** (*cakkhāyatana*), etc., whatever should be said has all been said already in the *Visuddhimagga* in the Description of the Aggre-

gates and in the Description of the Bases (XIV, 37-52; XV, 1-16).

With the arising of mentality-materiality (*nāmarūpa-samudayā*): But here the arising of the sixfold base should be understood to occur from the arising of mentality-materiality according to the method stated in the *Visuddhimagga* in the Description of Dependent Arising, as to which mentality, which materiality, and which mentality-materiality are a condition for which base (XVII, 206-219).

Mentality-Materiality

54. In the section on mentality-materiality, **mentality** (*nāma*) has the characteristic of bending (*namana*); **materiality** (*rūpa*) has the characteristic of being molested (*ruppana*).[53] In the detailed section, however, **feeling** (*vedanā*) is to be understood as the feeling aggregate, **perception** (*saññā*) as the perception aggregate, and **volition, contact and attention** (*cetanā phasso manasikāro*) as the formations aggregate. While it is certainly the case that other states are included in the formations aggregate, still these three are found in all classes of consciousness, even the weakest. That is why the formations aggregate is here pointed out only by means of these three.

The four great elements (*cattāri mahābhūtāni*): this is a designation for the four—earth, water, fire and air. The reason why these are called "great elements," and other determinations concerning them, are all stated in the *Visuddhimagga* in the Description of the Materiality Aggregate.[54]

Derived from the four great elements (*catunnañ ca mahābhūtānaṁ upādāya*): **derived from** (*upādāya*) = having clung to (*upādāyitvā*); "having grasped" is the meaning. Some also say "depending upon" (*nissāya*). And here the reading is completed by adding the word "existing" (*vattamānaṁ*). The Pali uses the genitive (in the term for the elements) in the sense of a group.

Hence the meaning here should be understood thus: the materiality that exists derived from the group of the four great elements.

Thus materiality taken altogether is to be understood as consisting of all the following: the four great elements beginning with the earth element, and the materiality that exists derived from the four great elements, stated in the canonical Abhidhamma to be of twenty-three kinds by analysis into the eye-base, etc.[55]

With the arising of consciousness (*viññāṇasamudayā*): But here the arising of mentality-materiality should be understood to occur with the arising of consciousness according to the method stated in the *Visuddhimagga* in the Description of Dependent Arising, as to which consciousness is a condition for which mentality, for which materiality, and for which mentality-materiality (XVII, 186-202). The rest by the method stated.

Consciousness

58. In the section on consciousness, **eye-consciousness** (*cakkhuviññāṇa*) is consciousness in the eye or consciousness born from the eye. So also with ear-, nose-, tongue- and body-consciousness. But with the other one, i.e. **mind-consciousness** (*manoviññāṇa*), mind itself is consciousness. This is a designation for the resultant consciousness of the three (mundane) planes of existence except for the two groups of fivefold consciousness.[56]

With the arising of formations (*saṅkhārasamudayā*): But here the arising of consciousness should be understood to occur with the arising of formations according to the method stated in the *Visuddhimagga*, as to which formation is a condition for which consciousness (XVII, 175-185).

Formations

62. In the section on formations, a **formation** (*saṅkhāra*) has

the characteristic of forming (*abhisaṅkharaṇalakkhaṇa*). But in the detailed section, **the bodily formation** (*kāyasaṅkhāra*) is a formation that proceeds from the body. This is a designation for the twenty kinds of bodily volition—the eight sense-sphere wholesome and twelve unwholesome—that occur by way of activation in the bodily door.[57] **The verbal formation** (*vacīsaṅkhāra*) is a formation that proceeds from speech. This is a designation for the (same) twenty kinds of verbal volition that occur by way of breaking into speech in the door of speech. **The mental formation** (*cittasaṅkhāra*) is a formation that proceeds from the mind. This is a designation for the twenty-nine kinds of mental volition—the mundane wholesome and unwholesome—that occur in one sitting alone in thought, and which do not cause activation of the bodily and verbal doors.[58]

With the arising of ignorance (*avijjāsamudayā*): But here ignorance should be understood as a condition for the wholesome by way of decisive support and for the unwholesome by way of conascence as well. The rest by the method stated.

Ignorance

66. In the section on ignorance, **not knowing about suffering** (*dukkhe aññāṇaṁ*) means not knowing about the truth of suffering. This is a designation for delusion (*moha*). The same method with respect to "not knowing about the origin of suffering," and so on.

Herein, not knowing about suffering should be understood in four ways: as to containment (*antogadhato*), as to physical basis (*vatthuto*), as to object (*ārammaṇato*), and as to concealment (*paṭicchādanato*). Thus, because of being included in the truth of suffering, it ("not knowing" or ignorance) is contained in suffering; and the truth of suffering is its physical basis by being its support condition; and (the truth of suffering) is its object by being its object condition; and it conceals the truth of suffering by preventing the penetration of its real characteristic and by not allowing knowledge to occur in regard to it.

Not knowing about the origin (of suffering) should be understood in three ways: as to physical basis, as to object, and as to concealment. And not knowing about cessation and the way (to cessation) should be understood in one way only: as to concealment. For non-knowledge only conceals cessation and the way by preventing the penetration of their real characteristics and by not allowing knowledge to occur in regard to them. But it is not contained in them because it is not included in this pair of truths. And these two truths are not its physical basis because they are not conascent. Nor are they its object because of its non-occurrence on account of them. For the last pair of truths are difficult to see because of their profundity, and non-knowledge, which is blind, does not occur there. But the first (pair of truths) is profound in the sense of opposition because of the difficulty in seeing the characteristic of their intrinsic nature; it occurs there by way of obsession by the perversions.

Furthermore: **About suffering** (*dukkhe*): to this extent ignorance is indicated as to inclusion, as to physical basis, as to object, and as to function. **About the origin of suffering** (*dukkhasamudaye*): to this extent, as to basis, as to object, and as to function. **About the cessation of suffering** (*dukkhanirodhe*) and **about the way leading to the cessation of suffering** (*dukkhanirodhagāminiyā paṭipadāya*): to this extent, as to function. But without distinction, (in each instance) ignorance is described in terms of its intrinsic nature by the phrase "not knowing."

With the arising of the taints (*āsavasamudayā*): But here the taint of sensual desire and the taint of being are conditions for ignorance by way of conascence, etc.; the taint of ignorance, only by way of decisive support. And here the ignorance that had arisen previously should be understood as the taint of ignorance. That is a decisive support condition for the ignorance that arises subsequently. The rest by the method stated.

The Taints

70. In the section on the taints, **with the arising of ignorance** (*avijjāsamudayā*): Here ignorance is a condition for the taint of sensual desire and the taint of being by way of decisive support, etc.; (it is a condition) for the taint of ignorance only by way of decisive support. And here the ignorance that arises subsequently should be understood as the taint of ignorance. The previously arisen ignorance itself becomes a decisive support condition for the subsequently arisen taint of ignorance. The rest by the aforesaid method.

This section is stated by way of showing the condition for the ignorance which heads the factors of dependent arising. Stated thus, the undiscoverability (*anamataggatā*) of any beginning of *saṁsāra* is established. How? Because with the arising of the taints there is the arising of ignorance, and with the arising of ignorance there is the arising of the taints. Thus the taints are a condition for ignorance, and ignorance is a condition for the taints. Having shown this, (it follows that) no first point of ignorance is manifest, and because none is manifest the undiscoverability of any beginning of *saṁsāra* is proven.[59]

Conclusion

Thus in all this sutta **sixteen sections** have been stated: the section on the courses of kamma, the section on nutriment, the section on suffering, and the sections on ageing and death, birth, being, clinging, craving, feeling, contact, the sixfold base, mentality-materiality, consciousness, formations, ignorance and the taints.

As to these, in each individual section there is a twofold analysis—in brief and in detail—amounting to thirty-two cases. Thus in this sutta, in these thirty-two cases, the Four (Noble) Truths are expounded. Among these, in the sixteen cases stated in detail, Arahantship is expounded.

But according to the opinion of the Elder, the four truths and the four paths are expounded in the thirty-two cases.[60] Thus in the entire Word of the Buddha comprised in the five great Nikāyas, there is no sutta except for this Discourse on Right View where the Four (Noble) Truths are explained thirty-two times and where Arahantship is explained thirty-two times.

That is what the Venerable Sāriputta said (*idam avoc'āyasmā Sāriputto*): The Venerable Sāriputta spoke this Discourse on Right View, having adorned it with sixty-four divisions—thirty-two expositions of the four truths and thirty-two expositions of Arahantship. The bhikkhus were satisfied and delighted in the Venerable Sāriputta's words.

In the *Papañcasūdanī*, the Commentary to the Majjhima Nikāya, the Explanation of the Discourse on Right View is concluded.

NOTES

1. The term *sammādiṭṭhi* is ordinarily used to mean simply a state, the path factor of right view. Here, however, the Pali expression is used as a masculine noun to mean, in the first instance, a person possessing right view; hence it has been rendered "one of right view." The commentator contrasts this unusual usage of the term with the more common usage where *sammādiṭṭhi* signifies a state (*dhamma*), that is, the path factor rather than the individual endowed with that state.

2. The knowledge of kamma as one's own (*kammassakatañāṇa*) is often expressed in the Suttas thus: "I am the owner of my kamma, the heir of my kamma, I spring from my kamma, I am bound to my kamma, I have kamma as my refuge. Whatever kamma I perform, good or bad, of that I am the heir." In short, it is knowledge of the moral efficacy of action, of the fact that one's willed deeds fashion one's destiny. Knowledge in conformity with the truths (*saccānulomikañāṇa*) is conceptual knowledge of the Four Noble Truths, accompanied by understanding and acceptance of them.

3. The understanding or wisdom (*paññā*) connected with the paths and fruits is supramundane because its object is the supramundane *dhamma*, Nibbāna, and because it leads to the overcoming of the world.

4. A disciple in higher training (*sekha*) is one at any of the three lower levels of sanctity—a stream-enterer, once-returner, or non-returner—or one who has reached their respective paths. His right view is said to be fixed in destiny (*niyata*) because it necessarily leads to final liberation.

5. The "one beyond training" (*asekha*) is the Arahant, so called because he has completed the threefold training in virtue, concentration and wisdom.

6. The ninefold supramundane Dhamma: the four paths, the four fruitions, and Nibbāna.

7. The interpretation of "the bhikkhus" and "the Elder" is offered by Sub. Cy., which also presents an alternative interpretation, based on the commentary to the Vatthupama Sutta (M.7) according to which the bhikkhus are the pupils of the Elder Mahāsangharakkhita and "the Elder" is the Elder Mahāsangharakkhita.

8. See commentary to the third *pārājikā* offence.

9. See commentary to the second *pārājikā* offence.

10. The meaning of several of these terms, obscure in the original Pali, has been elaborated with the aid of the Sub. Cy.

11. Consent (*adhivāsana*) is included to cover the case where one of the partners is initially an unwilling victim of another's assault, but during the course of union consents to the act and thereby becomes a participant.

12. These are references to the two great classics of Hindu India, the *Mahābhārata* and the *Rāmāyana*.

13. Wrong views of fixed destiny (*niyatā micchādiṭṭhi*) are views which deny the moral efficacy of action or which tend to undermine the foundations of morality. For the most common examples, see D.2/i, 52-56, and M.76/i, 515-18.

14. The chief factor in the first seven courses of kamma is volition; the other three courses are identical with the mental factors of greed, hatred and wrong view, which are associated with volition in the states of consciousness in which they arise.

15. This refers to the Abhidhamma classification of consciousness, according to which wholesome sense-sphere con-

sciousness is of eight types, four associated with knowledge, four dissociated from knowledge. The abstinences, according to the Abhidhamma, occur in sense-sphere consciousness only one at a time on occasions when one deliberately abstains from some wrong. In supramundane consciousness all three abstinences—right speech, right action and right livelihood—occur together simultaneously.

16. Right view is synonymous with the mental factor of wisdom (*paññā*) or non-delusion (*amoha*); it is always accompanied by the other two wholesome roots, though the latter do not necessarily occur in conjunction with right view.

17. Literally, or in the strict sense (*nippariyāyena*), only covetousness and greed, being synonyms of craving (*taṇhā*), count as the origin of suffering. But in a looser or figurative manner of exposition (*pariyāyena*) all the roots are the truth of the origin, since as roots of kamma they help to sustain the round of rebirth and suffering.

18. The guideline of conversion (*āvattahāra*) is one of the methods of deduction in the exegetical guide, the *Nettippakaraṇa*. According to this guideline, an expositor of a sutta is to extract from a particular text a standard doctrinal concept belonging to a dichotomy, and then taking this concept as a basis, he is to show that the other member of the dichotomy is also implied by the passage under consideration, and therefore "turns up" when the first member is mentioned.

19. The path of non-return (*anāgāmimagga*) is stated because this path eradicates all sensual lust and aversion.

20. The path of Arahantship is implied by the eradication of conceit and ignorance and by the arousing of true knowledge.

21. The verb *āharati* normally means "to bring," but here it is rendered as "nourish" to underscore its connection with *āhāra*, nutriment.

22. On the four *yoni* or modes of generation, see M.12/i, 73.

23. According to the Abhidhamma, the nutriment proper is the material phenomenon called nutritive essence (*ojā*), while the solid food ingested is the mere "basis" (*vatthu*) of the nutritive essence.

24. The point is that while in conventional terms food substances are distinguished as gross or subtle, this distinction is made in terms of the physical base only. The Abhidhamma classifies nutritive essence as subtle materiality (*sukhumarūpa*); it contrasts with gross materiality (*oḷārikarūpa*), which includes only the five sense organs and their objects.

25. This is the highest realm among the sense-sphere heavens. Above this come the Brahma realms, where physical nutriment is non-existent.

26. This is the simplest kind of material group (*rūpakalāpa*) recognized by the Abhidhamma theory of matter. It consists of the four primary elements, along with colour, smell, taste, and nutritive essence. All the more complex material groups also contain these eight phenomena as their foundation. Material groups in a living organism require an input of nutriment in order to endure in continuity.

27. Conascence condition (*sahajātapaccaya*) is the condition whereby the conditioning state contributes to the arising or maintenance of another state, the conditionally arisen state, when the latter arises simultaneously with itself. Consciousness is a conascence condition for the three other mental aggregates—feeling, perception and mental formations—both at rebirth and during the course of life. At rebirth it is also a conascence condition for the "triple continuity," i.e. the three material decads of body-sensitivity, sexual determination and the heart-base. Each of these consists of the above-mentioned eight material units along with physical life and, as the tenth factor, the material phenomenon after which it is named.

28. Kammically acquired materiality (*upādinnarūpa*) is matter that is born of kamma. It includes the physical sense faculties, the life faculty, masculinity, femininity, and the coexisting material phenomena in the same group. Though such types of matter are produced by kamma rather than by nutriment, they require nutriment to sustain them in continuity.

29. The Lakkhaṇa Saṁyutta (S.19/ii, 254-62) describes the torments experienced by beings in the realm of the petas or "afflicted spirits."

30. These similes are taken from the Puttamaṁsa Sutta, the Discourse on Son's Flesh (S.12:63/ii, 97-100). See Nyanaponika Thera, *The Four Nutriments of Life* (BPS Wheel No. 104/105, 1967), pp. 19-40, for the sutta along with its commentary.

31. A *yojana* is about seven miles.

32. The cow-observance and the dog-observance are forms of self-mortification which ascetics of the Buddha's time practised in the hope of purification; see M.57/i, 387. Apparently, women also observed them for short periods in the hope they would make them fertile.

33. The commentary to the Puttamaṁsa Sutta develops this analogy in greater detail than the present commentary.

34. The sutta elaborates as follows: If the cow stands, the creatures in the air attack it; if it leans against a wall, the creatures in the wall attack it; if it lies down, the creatures in the ground attack it; if it enters a pool of water, the creatures in the water attack it.

35. Contact arises from the coming together of an object, a physical basis or sense faculty (*vatthu*), and the corresponding type of consciousness.

36. The simile as given in the sutta is this: Two strong men grab hold of a weaker man by both arms and drag him towards a blazing charcoal pit. He wriggles and struggles to get free

because he knows that if he is thrown into the pit, he will meet death or deadly pain.

37. The king's men arrest a thief and bring him before the king. The king orders him struck with a hundred spears in the morning, another hundred at noon, and a third hundred in the evening. The man survives but experiences deadly pain.

38. See note 27.

39. The eight types of consciousness accompanied by greed are distinguished by the presence or absence of wrong view, by their accompanying feeling which may be pleasant or neutral, and by whether they are spontaneous or prompted.

40. The principle of the Four Noble Truths can be discerned in the format of the exposition: a particular item X, the arising of X, the cessation of X, and the way to the cessation of X.

41. In Pali the repetition *tesaṁ tesaṁ*, lit. "of them, of them," is understood to imply complete inclusiveness. The same applies to *tamhi tamhi*, "in that, in that," just below.

42. Whereas the previous definitions were framed in conventional terminology, those valid in the ultimate sense (*paramatthato*) define their subject solely in terms of "ultimate realities" such as aggregates and sense bases.

43. The various realms of existence are analyzed as threefold on the basis of the number of aggregates existing there. One-constituent being is the non-percipient realm (*asaññibhūmi*), which includes only the aggregate of material form. Four-constituent being is the four immaterial realms, which contain the four mental aggregates but not the aggregate of material form. Five-constituent being comprises all other realms, in which all five aggregates are present.

44. It seems that in the sense-sphere heavens, at death the beings simply dissipate into thin air, without leaving behind any corpse.

45. Decisive support condition (*upanissayapaccaya*) and conascence condition (*sahajātapaccaya*) are the two chief conditions among the twenty-four conditions of the *Paṭṭhāna* or Abhidhammic system of conditional relations. Decisive support holds between a conditioning state and a conditioned state that it helps to arise across an interval of time. Conascence condition holds between a conditioning state and a conditioned state that arise simultaneously. See also note 27 above.

46. Clinging to rituals and observances and clinging to a doctrine of self are both types of wrong view, but as they are enumerated as individual kinds of clinging in their own right, they are not included under clinging to views.

47. See above, note 32.

48. These are conditional relations that hold between successive mind-moments in the javana phase of a single cognitive process (*cittavīthi*).

49. Resultant feeling alone is intended here because this is an exposition of the round of existence, and in the formula of dependent arising the factors from consciousness through feeling are classified as the resultant phase of the round.

50. The two eye-consciousness elements are the wholesome-resultant and the unwholesome-resultant; the two resultant mind elements are the wholesome-resultant and the unwholesome-resultant receiving consciousness (*sampaṭicchanacitta*); the three resultant mind-consciousness elements are three types of investigating consciousness (*santīraṇacitta*).

51. The registration consciousness (*tadārammaṇacitta*) is a resultant type of consciousness that occurs through any of the sense doors. Its function is to register the datum that had been the object of the preceding javana series. The rebirth, life-continuum (*bhavaṅga*) and death consciousnesses are resultants that are considered to be "doorless" (*advārika*) because they occur at

an inner subliminal level, not through the intercourse of sense organs and sense objects.

52. This refers to the Abhidhamma classification of thirty-two types of resultant consciousness, of which twenty-two remain besides the ten types of sense-consciousness, five resultants of the unwholesome and five of the wholesome. The details are not necessary here.

53. These two definitions involve word plays difficult to reproduce in English. Ven. Ñāṇamoli has a note suggesting, half flippantly, "minding" for *namana* and "mattering" for *ruppana*.

54. In fact the *Visuddhimagga* discusses the four great elements not in its chapter on the Description of the Aggregates (Ch. XIV), but in the chapter on the meditation subject called the definition of the elements (Ch. XI).

55. Some instances of derived materiality are: the five sense faculties, colour, sound, smell, taste, the life faculty, sexual determination, nutritive essence, space, etc.

56. The three planes of existence were enumerated in §30. Only resultant consciousness is taken into account here because this is an exposition of the round.

57. The figures for the types of consciousness again come from the Abhidhamma. These types of consciousness can come to expression either through the door of bodily action or the door of speech, or they can remain within and not gain outer expression.

58. The nine types of volition which do not come to expression by body or speech are the five volitions of the five fine-material-sphere jhānas and the four of the four immaterial-sphere jhānas.

59. Elsewhere the Buddha says: "A first point of ignorance cannot be discovered, of which it can be said: Before that there was no ignorance and it came to be after that" (A.10:61/v,113).

In that sutta the Buddha cites the five hindrances as the condition for ignorance, but as these in turn presuppose ignorance, the vicious cycle is again established.

60. For the identity of the dissenting Elder, see §3 and note 7.

THE TRANSLATOR

Bhikkhu Ñāṇamoli was born in England in 1905 and graduated from Exeter College, Oxford. In 1948 he came to Sri Lanka, where he was ordained the following year at the Island Hermitage near Dodanduwa. During his 11 years in the Sangha Ven. Ñāṇamoli translated into lucid English some of the most difficult texts of Theravada Buddhism. In 1960, on one of his rare outings from the Hermitage, he suddenly passed away due to heart failure.

THE EDITOR

Bhikkhu Bodhi is a Buddhist monk of American nationality, born in New York City in 1944. After completing a doctorate in philosophy at Claremont Graduate School, he came to Sri Lanka in 1972, and was ordained the same year under the eminent scholar-monk, Ven. Balangoda Ananda Maitreya. Since 1984 he has been Editor for the Buddhist Publication Society, and its President since 1988.

Of related interest

THE DISCOURSE ON THE FRUITS OF RECLUSESHIP

The Sāmaññaphala Sutta and its Commentaries

Translated from the Pali by
Bhikkhu Bodhi

The Sāmaññaphala Sutta, The Discourse on the Fruits of Recluseship, is one of the most elevating of the Buddha's discourses. On a full-moon night in autumn, in reply to a question asked by King Ajātasattu of Magadha, the Buddha expounds the visible fruits of the Buddhist monk's life, sketching the progress of the disciple from his first steps on the path to the attainment of Nibbāna. The work is not only a great spiritual classic, but also a literary gem distinguished by its beauty of poetic imagery. This book contains a complete translation of the Sāmaññaphala Sutta together with its authoritative commentary and selections from two subcommentaries.

THE BUDDHIST PUBLICATION SOCIETY

The BPS is an approved charity dedicated to making known the Teaching of the Buddha, which has a vital message for people of all creeds. Founded in 1958, the BPS has published a wide variety of books and booklets covering a great range of topics. Its publications include accurate annotated translations of the Buddha's discourses, standard reference works, as well as original contemporary expositions of Buddhist thought and practice. These works present Buddhism as it truly is—a dynamic force which has influenced receptive minds for the past 2500 years and is still as relevant today as it was when it first arose. A full list of our publications will be sent upon request with an enclosure of U.S. $1 or its equivalent to cover air mail postage. Write to:

The Hony. Secretary
BUDDHIST PUBLICATION SOCIETY
P.O. Box 61
54, Sangharaja Mawatha
Kandy Sri Lanka

THE BUDDHIST PUBLICATION SOCIETY

[illegible] dedicated to making known the Teaching of the Buddha, which has a vital message for [illegible].

Founded in [illegible], the BPS has published a wide variety of books and booklets covering a great range of topics. Its publications include accurate annotated translations of the Buddha's discourses, standard reference works, as well as original contemporary expositions of Buddhist thought and practice. These works present Buddhism as it truly is — a dynamic force which has influenced receptive minds for the past 2500 years and is still as relevant today as it was when it first arose. A full list of our publications will be sent upon request with an enclosure of U.S. $1.00 or its equivalent to cover air mail postage. Write to:

The Hony. Secretary
BUDDHIST PUBLICATION SOCIETY
P.O. Box 61
54, Sangharaja Mawatha
Kandy • Sri Lanka